DESIGNER'S GUIDE TO

MAKING MONEY WITH·YOUR DESKTOP COMPUTER

JACK NEFF

DESIGNER'S GUIDE TO

MAKING MONEY WITH·YOUR DESKTOP COMPUTER

JACK NEFF

NORTH LIGHT BOOKS

Cincinnati, Ohio

Designer's Guide to Making Money With Your Desktop Computer. Copyright © 1992
by Jack Neff. Printed and bound in the United States of America. All rights reserved.
No part of this book may be reproduced in any form or by any electronic or mechanical
means including information storage and retrieval systems without permission in writing
from the publisher, except by a reviewer, who may quote brief passages in a review.
Published by North Light Books, an imprint of F&W Publications, Inc., 1507 Dana
Avenue, Cincinnati, Ohio 45207. First edition.

96   95   94   93   92   5   4   3   2   1

Library of Congress Cataloging in Publication Data

Neff, Jack
     Designer's guide to making money with your desktop computer / Jack Neff.
        p.   cm.
     Includes index.
     ISBN 0-89134-439-X
   1. Desktop publishing—Vocational guidance. 2. Printing industry—Vocational
guidance. 3. Graphic arts—Vocational guidance. I. Title.
    Z286.F45N43   1991
    686.2'-2544023—dc20   92-17029
                                            CIP

Editorial Direction by Diana Martin
Edited by Mary Cropper
Designed by Paul Neff

The following page constitutes an extension of this copyright page.

Permissions

About the Author

Jack Neff is a free-lance business writer in Batavia, Ohio, who writes for newspapers and business and trade publications in addition to copywriting. His work has appeared in *HOW* and *The Atlanta Journal and Constitution*.

Acknowledgments

I'd like to thank the many designers and others whose advice and patience helped make this book possible, particularly: Brian Bauer, Brian Blanchette, Steve BonDurant, Pat Brooks, Robert Creager, Debbie and Wade Dent, Steve Diamond, Michael Feldman, George Fiala, Rebecca Lodge, Todd Maniscalco, Eric Otto, Gayle Owens, Lynne Perry, Kitty Ryan, Jane Scarano, Gail Silverman, Sharon Baldwin Sittner and Joel Williams. Special thanks to editors Mary Cropper, Perri Weinberg-Schenker and Sandy Grieshop for their guidance and hard work.

Dedication

To Glenda and Matthew

Contents

Chapter 3
How to Find Clients 48
How to identify the most likely markets for your talent and get work while avoiding blind alleys.

Chapter 4
The Business Side 78
How to plan, price your work, and navigate tax and legal channels successfully.

Introduction

The impact of the computer on graphic design is still so recent that its full effects are unfolding. The basic hardware and software of the modern electronic studio, after all, are little more than a decade old. One thing is clear though: Desktop design and publishing are growing. Despite the prevalence of in-house graphic artists using desktop computers, thousands of designers are using their computers to make good incomes and enjoy entrepreneurial independence.

Though it's still in its formative ages, graphics computing is out of its infancy. That means the novelty is gone. Billing your services as "desktop design or publishing" once may have brought puzzled looks from customers. Now, the term is so commonplace it's almost meaningless. "Desktop publisher" is a label that might be worn by print shop employees making close to minimum wage, executives churning out glorified spreadsheets and genuine graphic designers.

Your new challenge is to compete in a world where more and more people think knowing how to operate a computer makes them designers. That means positioning yourself apart from the growing crowd of desktop publishers. It also means knowing where and how to find the most promising opportunities, and it means using your equipment purchases and business strategy to make the most of your money and talent.

This book is designed to help you do that. If you're setting up a desktop design and publishing business, this book will help you make the important early decisions that will shape your future. This book also will show you how your computer can improve your existing business.

First, the book covers how to make the most of your investment dollar when buying new equipment or upgrading your current toolbox. It also helps explore the essential issues in other areas of finding and outfitting your work space. Next, you'll get a closer look at how computers shape the available opportunities and at how and where you can develop profitable niches. You'll also see some successful strategies for identifying and landing potential clients in whatever specialty you develop. Finally, the book will help you handle tough business issues such as pricing, planning your business's future, and negotiating complicated tax and legal channels so you can keep the most of what you make.

Combined with your talent, this book can provide the information that will make your business a success.

Chapter One

Setting Up Shop

Deciding which computer equipment to buy is one of the most bewildering choices you'll face. The choices are seemingly endless. If you start with a computer you already own, at least the first choice is a little easier: Keep your existing computer, or trade it in for a more powerful one.

Getting the right equipment means more than hitting the neighborhood computer stores with a shopping list. Your computer dealer may know a lot about the needs of a desktop designer and publisher—or be totally ignorant. Either way, you'll be better prepared if you've done some homework before you start getting tossed around by one sales pitch after another. Analyzing the "state of the art" in graphics computing also should help you decide whether you want to buy new equipment, upgrade what you've already got or stand pat.

Your decisions should be based on more than the relative merits of the hardware and software that are available. The kind of work you plan to do and the clients you hope to attract should influence your choices more than anything else.

If you plan to produce newsletters with only spot color, it makes little sense to spend $6,000 or more for a high-end color video system with 19-inch monitor and 24-bit color. On the other hand, you'd be hard pressed to edit color images on a Macintosh Classic.

Here are some steps to take before you buy:

1. Define your business. Consider what kind of work you do, or may do in the future, and what kind of equipment you'll need to do it. If you're starting a new business, put out feelers to potential clients to get an idea of what kind of jobs might be available to you, so you'll know what capabilities you need.

2. Hit the library and the magazine rack. Get the current issues of the leading desktop design and publishing and computer magazines, and read them thoroughly to find out what's new from hardware and software vendors. Go to a library and get the past year's back issues, too. That should give you a complete cycle of reviews of the key hardware and software products. Once you get up to speed, stay there by subscribing to computer magazines. Buying

equipment is not a one-shot deal if you're going to be in business more than a few years.

3. Consider professional help. Check the Business-to-Business Yellow Pages in your area for listings of computer training consultants. Some of them also provide equipment selection advice. Try to find one who specializes in working with graphic artists and designers. Check with local desktop designers and publishers for referrals, too. You can expect to pay up to $100 an hour or more, but if you've narrowed yourself to very specific questions, it won't cost much compared to the thousands you'll spend on your equipment.

4. Make an equipment acquisition plan. Do you need the best video graphics system, scanner and laser printer right away? Or would it make sense to start with the computer system and a basic printer and add more expensive peripherals later? Draw up a strategy for acquiring equipment as your business grows. Make sure the equipment you buy early can expand to match the needs you identify in the future.

Adding a Computer to an Existing Design Studio

Computerizing an existing graphic arts studio or business may not be as dramatic a move as starting a desktop design and publishing business. But it's a lot more complicated than just plugging in a computer and training employees.

The most disruptive influence computers have on an existing operation is the way they compress several job duties into one. Suddenly, design, layout, illustration, typesetting, paste-up, proofreading and even color pre-press work can be compressed into one tool with one operator. A half-dozen or more separate job titles could become the realm of one employee.

In small operations, all of those duties may have been handled by one or two employees or partners. But in larger operations with more specialized job descriptions, there can be resistance to adding a computer. Designers may balk at taking on production tasks. Typesetters and paste-up artists may rightly perceive the computer as a threat to their jobs. And while owners may feel entitled to all the cost savings from increased productivity, employees may

Adding Computers Shrinks Staff

Steve BonDurant and Keith Meehan got their introduction to computers when their old employer, a now-defunct Rochester, New York, ad agency, sent them to an exhibition to learn about them. The agency decided to stick with traditional typesetting for most of its work. But when the company folded a year later, Bon Durant and Meehan knew their work would one day center around computers.

The two founded Icon Graphics Inc. in May 1988. They worked with several former clients of their old employer and specialized in packaging design and electronic illustration. For the first seven months, they operated without computers. But BonDurant contacted a friend who operates a computer graphics and training facility and got advice about what to buy and how to set it up. In January 1989, they leased a Macintosh II to minimize their initial outlay.

"At first we just used it for typesetting and thought we were pretty hot stuff if we could rotate the type," BonDurant says. "Now we do logos, hand-rendered type and a lot of illustrations—just about everything."

But the transition didn't happen overnight—or painlessly. Icon had seven employees before adding the computer. Two years later, only BonDurant and Meehan were left. Part of the reason, BonDurant says, was the toll the recession took on product introductions and packaging. But computerization played another big part.

"As we used the Mac more, our efficiency got to be a lot greater," BonDurant says. "We found that we outgrew our staff. It was just too expensive to train people, and the people we were trying to train just couldn't roll with the efficiency or the new way of doing things." Taking the place of some employees now are contractors with their own equipment and their own responsibility for training.

Besides changing Icon's work force, the computer also changed Icon's rates. The company started with a structure adapted from the ad agency, which included different rates for conceptual work, design development, prototype production and general work, such as meetings and phone calls. Icon added a "Mac rate" for time spent on the computer because it didn't fit into the other categories, BonDurant says.

"It's our highest rate because of the increased productivity of working on the Mac," BonDurant says. "We try to compare it to how much it would cost to do the same things conventionally."

To train themselves on the Mac, BonDurant and Meehan have tried to take things in small bites. They've concentrated on three software packages: FreeHand for illustration and packaging design, QuarkXPress for page layout and Adobe Photoshop for color image editing (though Icon uses a color pre-press house for color proofing as well as scans and imagesetting).

"We've tried to make a choice in software and dedicate all our time to learning one program in each area," BonDurant says. "A lot of our clients have purchased every single piece of software they've ever heard of but don't know how to use any of them. That doesn't really make sense financially or otherwise."

Icon also has added more hardware in bite-size chunks. It has two Mac SE/30s with standard color monitors and 24-bit color for high-end packaging work. The studio also has a Mac Plus for strictly administrative work. Each purchase was made after checking the options with a consultant. "A consultant is a very valuable tool," BonDurant says. "They're worth the fees in the time they save you in making a decision and avoiding mistakes."

He says Icon's only equipment mistake was leasing a stat camera, which the studio seldom uses. When the lease expires, BonDurant plans to replace the camera's capital expense with a scanner, for which he sees much more use.

feel differently. Is it fair to ask employees to take on more duties and learn new skills without getting paid more?

Adding a computer also changes the kind of work you handle. You may have been going to outside vendors for typesetting and paste-up in the past. Now you do that in-house. But just adding the computer doesn't automatically give you typographic skills. Getting a color imaging program may give you the potential to process film and do color separations. But it doesn't give you the skills and experience of a color prepress house. Your in-house training may need to include more than simple computer and software skills. And the efficiency and economics of handling more tasks in-house could make your business more production-oriented and less design-oriented than you ever imagined.

Also, count on adjusting your rate structure to account for the changes a computer makes. You may have had one rate for conceptual time, one for design time, and another for employees' production time. Even if one person did all those things in the past, they were at least distinct functions that were relatively easy to track. How do you account for them separately when one person performs all three functions — some of them almost simultaneously — with the same equipment?

Some studios answer the question by creating a blended rate for computer time that averages all functions into account. Others still bill them separately. But either way, rates should be bumped up. Otherwise, studios won't reap any of the benefits from increased productivity.

PC vs. Mac: Being On the Right Platform

The choice between PC and Mac was once clear-cut. PCs were economical if hard-to-use workhorses for left-brained folks who wanted to crunch numbers and process words. They were strictly for low-end graphics applications and two colors at best. Macs were friendly computers for graphic artists and desktop designers and publishers. But before you dump your PC to do design, or decide that your Mac can't handle heavy-duty word processing and data manipulation, take another look at the current sit-

uation. In recent years, the distinctions have blurred. Lower-priced Macs, like the Classic and LC lines, are comparable in price and capability to PC counterparts. Microsoft's Windows brought the "point-and-click" ease of Apple operating systems to the PC platform. And graphics software for PCs have improved, too.

The wall between PCs and Macs is going the way of the Berlin Wall. Newer Macs have superdrives that can translate most files to be PC-readable. Fairly inexpensive software will do the same job. And if you don't have either, service bureaus can reconfigure files for a nominal charge. The future promises even more convergence. IBM and Apple are collaborating to set a single industry standard for operating systems and applications. And graphics software for existing PC systems keeps improving.

Another factor to consider in choosing a platform is what you are already using. It may not make sense to learn a whole new system. Also consider what your clients are likely to use. If your business is primarily typesetting and production for corporate clients, operating on PC software is a plus. Translating files from Mac to PC or from one word processing system to another is possible, but it's still time-consuming and somewhat error-prone. If you plan to work with graphic designers or higher-end users, on the other hand, a Mac seems almost a must. The prejudices here are strong. Even designers who don't use computers think "Mac" when they think computers. Fair or not, using a PC could undermine your credibility.

How Much — and What — Equipment Is Enough for You?

Your computer system is the most important, and expensive, choice you'll make. But being cheap now can cost you later. The bargain-priced Mac Classic and Classic II, for instance, offer very limited expandability and only support a monochrome monitor. And they're excruciatingly slow for graphics applications. If you want a color monitor, you'll need to move up to an LC and kick in about $500 more. The LC has one expansion slot, and it's twice as fast as a Classic. But many desktop publishers and designers consider the Classic and LC lines too slow for graphics and page layout duties.

For the best results, Mac designers prefer the SE/30, II, IIsi, IIci and IIfx models. The SE/30 and IIsi are slow for graphics applications, but they can be upgraded to match higher-priced models for speed. You also can get an accelerator card for your old Mac Plus to bring it up to speed, though it's still more limited than SE/30s and up. Generally, designers use II-and-up models, which allow ready upgradability. Some have had luck with SE/30 upgrades, but those limit your ability to match the speed and video capabilities of the highest-end Macs.

Here are some speed comparisons to consider:

1. The SE/30 and IIsi are 25 percent faster than an LC.
2. The IIci is another 25 percent faster.
3. The IIfx is a whopping 60 percent faster than the IIci and five times faster than the Classic.

Most designers have taken a wait-and-see attitude with the Quadra. Early compatibility problems with Quadras and Apple's own software made them a headache for many users, though those will likely be ironed out in later releases. The improvements in processing speed won't make that much difference to you unless you're a color shop working on monstrously large files.

On the PC side, the same trade-offs apply. Machines based on Intel's 8088 or 286 chips will do the job, but they're awfully slow compared to 386 and 486 machines. Clock speeds comparable to a Mac IIci are found in 386-based PCs.

The bottom line is that clients aren't likely to care how many megahertz your CPU operates at. They just care about the finished product. So if you're comfortable saving a few thousand bucks, and you're not interested in high-end color applications, you can get by with a low-priced computer.

But keep in mind that your comfort level may change. When you start, a slower machine may not seem that slow because you're not exactly up to speed, either. You'll get faster over time, but the computer won't. The result could be growing frustration.

The long view is also important. Cheaper

computers may limit your ability to upgrade in the future. It's wiser to save money on peripherals at first, because it's cheaper and easier to upgrade a monitor than buy a new computer system. Key questions to ask when buying your CPU are whether it will permit you to add improved chips, accelerator cards, random-access memory and video graphics cards in the future.

Working With Your Existing Equipment

When in doubt, never throw it out. Your existing computer system is always the place to start when considering how to outfit your design business. One good reason to hold onto your current equipment as long as you can is that competition in personal computers keeps driving prices down and delivering better value. If you can wait, or upgrade until you buy new, you may get a better deal down the road.

Even if you decide to buy a new machine, you can always use a backup system in case the new one needs to be serviced. And many designers find an older or lower-powered computer still has a place in the studio to handle bookkeeping or word processing. That's especially true if you want to bring a part-time employee or contractor in to handle those duties without tying up the graphics computer.

Your old computer could even turn out to be your future computer. The "box"—the shell that contains all the chips and boards that do the work—seldom wears out. And if you purchased wisely to start out with, you can probably buy CPU accelerators, video cards and other upgrades that will be cheaper than buying a whole new computer. The sum of a new system generally costs more than its parts.

"The nice thing about the Mac II and up is that the box is big enough to allow you to upgrade the motherboard, which will always be better than buying new," says Todd Maniscalco, president of the Waukesau, Wisconsin, consulting and training company Total Computer Graphics Inc. Taking into account price and future upgradability, he says, a IIci is probably the best buy.

One product, the Radius Rocket, appears to have gotten the bugs out after crashing and burning on its test launch. It can boost Mac II models to fx and above speeds. DayStar is another upgrade manufacturer Maniscalco recommends.

PC products also offer considerable potential for upgradability. Since the PC side has many key manufacturers instead of one, there's a wide variety of quality upgrade packages to choose from. But the PC models' lower prices make buying a whole new machine more attractive than with the higher-priced Macs.

One potential problem with upgrades that don't come from the original manufacturer is software compatibility. That leads many to stick with the tried-and-true upgrade packages. But upgrade products from the manufacturer — or even new computers — can run into that problem.

Because of their cost and potential problems, upgrade packages make poor candidates for mail order. Buying them from a dealer means you can run your software on the upgraded model at the showroom to find any compatibility problems. It also gives you an added layer of technical support. You'll want to use the dealer to at least look at the performance of the video card and monitor upgrade you buy, even if you purchase by mail order.

Your biggest gamble in upgrades is replacing the CPU motherboard. RAM chips are generally of uniform quality. And laser printers offer a host of upgrade features from their manufacturers that should allay concerns.

Hard Drive
The equipment-buying mistake desktop designers and publishers most often cite is not getting a big enough hard drive. And the standard configurations on Mac models usually come short of what you'll want in the long run.

Total Computer Graphics' Maniscalco recommends no less than 100MB for any graphics or desktop publishing applications and 300MB or more for color image editing. Less hard disk memory than that can quickly become inconvenient, given the size of graphics files.

"Get the best disk drive possible within your budget," Maniscalco says. "If your keyboard goes down, you can get another one. But if your hard disk goes down and the data is not backed up, you can't replace it." Apple's hard disks are in the medium range of quality, he says, and he

---

Cashing in on Caches

Disk-caching is one relatively cheap — albeit limited — way to increase the speed of even low-end systems. A disk cache is an area of the computer memory set aside for data you've already accessed, which makes software work much faster. Mac systems let you define cache size on the control panel. Microsoft offers the SMARTdrive disk-caching pro-.gram for Windows users, or you can buy software for disk-caching on PCs without Windows for less than $80. CPU accelerator cards are another option to boost older or slower machines. But since they start at $1,300, it doesn't cost much more to buy a better computer.

Higher-end systems (386 and up on the PC side and IIsi and up for Mac) can be sped up further with a RAM cache card, a feature that boosts system speed 20 to 40 percent for less than $200. A Mac IIsi with a RAM cache can be as fast as a IIci without one.

---

recommends going higher when possible. He rates hard drives made by CDC among the best. Some other companies, such as Microtech, sell a variety of manufacturers hard drives under their name. But you may be able to specify a CDC drive in your order.

Backup Storage
Even on a 100MB hard drive, you can't store everything you ever did. But backing up large jobs on diskettes is difficult or, for larger files, impossible. A system that will let you easily back up your work is vital. Tedium begets neglect, so don't assume you'll back up your work automatically.

One solution may be a CD-ROM drive, which is an external device that reads information on CDs rather than ordinary floppy disks. The advantage is that you can store many times more information on a CD than even the best floppy disk. A CD-ROM drive is a frill you may not want right away but should consider as your business matures.

A "streaming tape" system is another alternative that makes storing easier. Such systems save data continuously on cassettelike magnetic tape. But a better one may be a plug-in hard-drive cartridge, which may cost less and offer more. Unlike tape systems, a backup hard drive will preserve your data in the same structure you used in the first place. That eliminates the need to sort everything back into place when you restore data later on. The cartridge also gives you an emergency backup to use while your hard disk is in for repair.

Memory
As little as 2 megabytes of random-access memory is adequate for many tasks, particularly black-and-white or spot-color layouts. But 4MB will speed things up a lot for very little additional outlay. RAM upgrades cost less than $50 per megabyte, so they're one of the cheapest things you can buy to make your life easier. Graphics and page layout programs will slow down considerably if the computer has to keep shifting chunks of the program code from RAM to your hard drive. The extra RAM is especially helpful if you use a scanner or Windows.

All but the lowest-end systems should allow an upgrade to 8MB. You may want that or more for higher-end uses down the road, such as color image editing.

Video Display System
Keep in mind that upgrading the monitor may mean upgrading the video control card, particularly if you don't plan for the upgrade when you buy the system. And the card can cost as much as the monitor, or more. So if you can only afford monochrome now but may want to expand to color someday, consider investing in a card that can handle both at the outset.

You won't need 24-bit color unless you do color imaging, because 8-bit is perfectly adequate for one- or two-color work. And there's no point in getting 24-bit color if you don't need it, because it will only slow down your drawing or layout programs. Still, you may want to consider a card that will support both 8-bit and 24-bit color if you think you'd like to upgrade someday.

The choice of monitors is dizzyingly wide, especially on the Mac side. Evaluate monitors on both graphics and text before you buy. Cheaper models can look good for graphics but make many fonts extremely difficult to read. Nice options include Radius Pivot models that allow screens to be turned to vertical, horizontal or diagonal positions and two-page monitors, which are a big plus for multipage layouts. A full one-page or two-page monitor can save enough time in the long run to justify the cost.

Printer
Some kind of laser printer, at least capable of providing comps, is a must. Going to the service bureau for every comp gets to be a drag, even if it's next door.

You'll need a printer that uses the PostScript format to get the best graphic reproduction and maximum flexibility in font selection and type size. Expect to pay anywhere from $1,000 to $7,000, depending on speed, durability and quality of reproduction.

Volume is an important consideration for heavy users, but a small operation isn't likely to push even low-end models too hard. Low-end models print four pages per minute, while higher-end models handle up to eleven. More expensive models are designed to hold up under use as heavy as 20,000 pages per month.

A 300 dpi printer will do fine for comps and some low-end, text-intensive jobs. If you just want comps, a 400 dpi printer or above may be a waste of money. But if you have a lot of jobs that don't really need imagesetter quality for mechanicals, consider a 400 dpi printer. They provide four times the quality of 300 dpi and don't seem to have the problems that higher-resolution laser printers have.

Much has been made in recent years about how high-end laser printers, such as 600 dpi and 800 dpi models, will make typesetters obsolete. It hasn't happened yet. Users still report lots of problems with these laser printers; software has yet to provide flawless reproduction for many higher-resolution laser printers.

Color printers are a nice luxury for color comps, but they can't provide the kind of color output that will truly do a project justice. These are mainly the province of do-it-yourself executives working on business reports.

These illustrations show the differences in resolution among 300 dpi, 600 dpi and 1000 dpi laser printers as well as 1,270 dpi Linotronic output.

Goudy Bold

From top to bottom: Tints of black in increments of 10%; 1 pt., half-point and hairline rules; photograph scanned at 72 dpi; Goudy characters at 12, 10, 8 pts; diagonal rules.

ABCDEFGHIJKLMNOPQRSTUVWXYZ
abcdefghijklmnopqrstuvwxyz1234567890

ABCDEFGHIJKLMNOPQRSTUVWXYZ
abcdefghijklmnopqrstuvwxyz1234567890

ABCDEFGHIJKLMNOPQRSTUVWXYZ
abcdefghijklmnopqrstuvwxyz1234567890

300 dpi

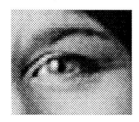

Goudy Bold

From top to bottom: Tints of black in increments of 10%; 1 pt., half-point and hairline rules; photograph scanned at 72 dpi; Goudy characters at 12, 10, 8 pts; diagonal rules.

ABCDEFGHIJKLMNOPQRSTUVWXYZ
abcdefghijklmnopqrstuvwxyz1234567890

ABCDEFGHIJKLMNOPQRSTUVWXYZ
abcdefghijklmnopqrstuvwxyz1234567890

ABCDEFGHIJKLMNOPQRSTUVWXYZ
abcdefghijklmnopqrstuvwxyz1234567890

600 dpi

Goudy Bold

From top to bottom: Tints of black in increments of 10%; 1 pt., half-point and hairline rules; photograph scanned at 72 dpi; Goudy characters at 12, 10, 8 pts; diagonal rules.

ABCDEFGHIJKLMNOPQRSTUVWXYZ
abcdefghijklmnopqrstuvwxyz1234567890

ABCDEFGHIJKLMNOPQRSTUVWXYZ
abcdefghijklmnopqrstuvwxyz1234567890

ABCDEFGHIJKLMNOPQRSTUVWXYZ
abcdefghijklmnopqrstuvwxyz1234567890

1000 dpi

Goudy Bold

From top to bottom: Tints of black in increments of 10%; 1 pt., half-point and hairline rules; photograph scanned at 72 dpi; Goudy characters at 12, 10, 8 pts; diagonal rules.

ABCDEFGHIJKLMNOPQRSTUVWXYZ
abcdefghijklmnopqrstuvwxyz1234567890

ABCDEFGHIJKLMNOPQRSTUVWXYZ
abcdefghijklmnopqrstuvwxyz1234567890

ABCDEFGHIJKLMNOPQRSTUVWXYZ
abcdefghijklmnopqrstuvwxyz1234567890

1,270 Linotronic output

Modem/Fax

A modem can save you lots of trips to the service bureau or even be a way to quickly get raw text from clients in or out of town. Even if you never use modems to send or receive work, they can open a world of information through on-line services and bulletin boards. Don't consider anything less than a 2,400-baud modem—you'll sacrifice much speed for savings of $100 or less. Even a 9,600-baud model costs only $200 to $300 more than a 2,400-baud. Poor phone lines may prevent you from taking full advantage of the higher speeds, but you can always downshift to 2,400 or 1,200 if there are problems.

A fax, or fax capability, is a must for any business these days, especially a design business. Stand-alone faxes can be had for less than $500 if you have simple needs. But more fully featured plain-paper faxes costing hundreds more are worth the investment if you have the money.

You may want a fax/modem that can send files from your computer to a fax machine and receive faxed documents into your computer system. It will do all the work of a modem and much of the work of a fax for about $100 more than a plain modem, and $200 or so less than an external fax. It can also save you the time and expense of printing out a file before sending it to a client to review. But a fax/modem does have disadvantages. If you want to fax hard copy and you don't have a scanner, you're out of luck. Even if you have a scanner, having to scan and then fax documents can get annoying if it happens too often.

Here's another interesting equipment combination to consider: Buy a fax/modem *and* an inexpensive fax machine. It will cost you only about $100 more than buying the fax and the modem separately. And you can easily use your fax as a low-end scanner.

Also, some higher-end fax/modems also include answering machines, which if nothing else could free up some room on your desk.

Scanner

For strictly typesetting applications, a relatively inexpensive optical character resolution (OCR) scanner can save hours of inputting hard copy. But the cost will pay for quite a few hours of typing, too—from $600 for a model capable of occasional use to $4,000 for one that handles high volumes. Other uses include inputting templates for forms, importing clip art or scanning photos. They're also used for placement purposes on comps.

Hand-held scanners come cheap—in the hundreds rather than thousands—but they severely limit your ability to capture larger graphics. To import photos or graphics, you'll pay around $2,000 for a better desktop grayscale or midrange color scanner. A color scanner that does justice to color photos and detailed illustrations costs $25,000 and up, so it's probably best left to the service bureau. And if your need to input type or capture graphics is slight, you can probably do without any kind of scanner.

Surge Protection

Surge protectors of some kind are important to protect your investment in equipment. Most of these use dollar-size disks called metal-oxide varistors (MOV) that channel a surge into the ground circuit and away from your computer. The drawback to MOVs is that they deteriorate. Some experts advise that the disks be replaced once a year. In case of a nearby lightning strike, they may end up diverting the surge from one part of your system to another.

More recent models, such as Zero Surge, don't use MOVs; instead, they channel the surge along the neutral wire. They cost three to seven times more than an MOV surge suppressor, but they're rated for ten years of useful life.

If you have a modem, don't forget to get a surge protector for the phone line leading into your computer. Lightning strikes on telephone lines also can cause surges that damage equipment and destroy data.

Standby Power Supplies and Undervoltage Protection

These devices sound nice in theory, but in practice you have to spend a lot of money to get one that does everything it should. The best idea is to save your work often. But if power is notoriously unreliable where you work, you may need more expensive protection. If you buy a power-maintenance system, test it to make sure it has enough power to come through in a pinch.

To preserve what's on your screen when power fails, an undervoltage protection system has to kick on in nanoseconds. Then it will sustain the computer until the battery is drained. An alarm sounds when the unit is out of power — usually a few minutes — giving you time to save your work. Units costing $200 and up may help during light-flickering outages. But to deal with rolling brownouts that plague users in some power-strapped communities, you'll need an uninterruptible power supply, which starts at $600. Remember, though, that even the best units won't get you through sustained power outages.

Software

Fortunately, the range of choices here is a lot narrower than for hardware. Most of the electronic design world is squared off into Adobe Illustrator or Aldus FreeHand camps for Mac drawing programs, with CorelDRAW! gaining a stronger position all the time. FreeHand and CorelDRAW! are the top drawing programs in a crowded field for Windows and DOS applications.

For page layout applications, Aldus PageMaker and QuarkXPress dominate on Macs; PageMaker and Ventura Publisher are the authorities for PCs. The paint and color image editing arena is a little more crowded, but Adobe Photoshop and Letraset ColorStudio come out on top for their adaptability in both color paint and image processing areas.

Each program has a loyal following and its own pros and cons. What's important to one user may be insignificant to another, depending on what kind of work they do. And all programs continually upgrade to overcome their shortcomings and competitors' strengths.

If you're already familiar with a program, stick with it. Its drawbacks aren't likely to be nearly as big as those of learning new software. But if you haven't chosen a program yet, research as much as you can before you buy. Read every magazine review you can find. Call customer support or inquiry numbers to pose your questions directly to the companies. The goal is to master the few programs you'll use without wasting money and time with programs you may not like.

Fonts

Fonts that come with your printer or are available from the printer vendor will do for many, if not most, jobs. You can get through other jobs with drawing programs that offer selections of fonts. But there will be projects that call for additional fonts, some of which you can create using drawing programs and fonts that come with your laser printer. Others you may have to buy, with mail order offering the best selection and prices.

You can get some fonts virtually free by obtaining screen fonts through the Adobe Forum on CompuServe or other bulletin boards. The screen fonts won't give you enough resolution for output, but you can then take your disk to a service bureau that has the font and get output for a fraction of the cost of buying an expensive set of fonts. It's a good option, especially for a one-time job.

Service Bureaus: Why You Need Them, How to Choose Them

No matter how much you plunk down for a computer system, you'll probably end up going to a service bureau for some things. Less-involved jobs may only require 300 dpi laser output. But you'll routinely use a service bureau for imagesetting or higher-end laser printing. Scanned images, halftones, photo stripping and color separations are among the other tasks that will lead you to develop a close relationship with your service bureau. In fact, selecting a service bureau is a key business decision. Here are some factors to consider:

■ *Value.* Price is always an important consideration. But if someone undercuts the competition significantly, you've got to wonder why.

■ *Location.* The closer the better, other things being equal. Even if you can send your work by modem, you'll still want to pick up the output. Courier fees can add up quickly. And if you have to drive an hour round trip to get there, don't forget how much your time is worth. Remember, each job could require at least two trips, and maybe a lot more.

It's usually wise to get a sample run out on an imagesetter before having the whole job output. Resolution differences between a laser printer and imagesetter make it hard to predict what the final output will look like before it's in your hand. You may want to adjust your file before getting the final mechanical — or show the client comps from the imagesetter before sticking your neck out on a final run.

■ *Compatibility*. The service bureau doesn't have to have the same software you do to output your files, but it sure helps. It's possible to have your PC file typeset by a PostScript device in a service bureau that has only Mac-literate employees; if there are glitches, though, you may get little help.

■ *Cooperation and attitude*. How flexible is your service bureau? Will it bill your clients directly rather than get payment from you up front, if that's the policy you prefer? How willing are employees to help you with your questions, especially if you're just starting out? Will they charge you consulting fees to answer those questions? What kind of turnaround time do they offer? Newer service bureaus may be hungry, and what they lack in experience they could make up for in attitude.

Finding the Best Deals on Hardware and Software

Most people go to computer dealers for big-ticket purchases, and with good reason. Sending thousands of dollars to a mail-order house for a computer system spooks the bravest of souls. The computer dealer, on the other hand, is down the street. You know where to find the culprit if there's trouble. And you can see what you're buying.

Unfortunately, you may end up paying a lot for that security. And it may not be that much better than what a reputable mail-order house provides. Better mail-order houses provide as much phone support as your computer dealer. People have even repaired equipment with phone instructions from mail-order houses — a level of advice you'd be hard-pressed to get from some computer dealers. And you can still scout the computer stores for demos before you buy.

Mail order gets a big piece of the action when it comes to software and peripherals, because

When It Pays to Buy Your Own Imagesetter

Relatively few desktop designers and publishers or small studios own their own imagesetting equipment. After all, the cost could equal or exceed many times what you invested in your other equipment. But buying your own imagesetter can pay off once you're established and have the financial means to buy or lease one.

"I was paying about $400 to $800 a month in service bureau charges, and that's about the break-even point where I could afford to buy a Linotronic," says Robert Creager, a Westerville, Ohio, designer (see case study, page 39). He bought a used L-100 and processor for $12,000, a big savings over the $50,000 to $75,000 for a new system. The hidden value in the purchase is the time your own imagesetter can save you. "If you're working with halftones, you don't always get what you want the first time through," Creager says. "It takes a lot of noodling and finagling. I was finding I was having to send jobs back for a second and third time. And for most of the accounts I work with, time is more important than money."

Thom Hartman, president of the Atlanta-based Newsletter Factory (see case study on pages 32-33), bought a Linotronic when his business still had only three employees. Today, he has fifteen employees and two Linotronics. "We used a service bureau for the first year we were in business and we decided it was crazy," he says. "Rarely have I seen a service bureau do the job right the first time. Then, we had the hassle of driving across town and waiting in line with other people, plus font and software incompatibility. We weren't doing enough volume of business to justify the cost of a Linotronic. But buying it early on saved us so much time. And that has a value."

buyers feel less risk on smaller-ticket items. A recent survey by *Macworld* found 85 percent of respondents had bought Mac-related products by mail. But only 4 percent of those customers bought computers that way, while 53 percent bought peripherals, 63 percent bought supplies and 94 percent bought software.

The same survey found 76 percent of mail-order buyers had never experienced problems. That may seem comforting at first, but a roughly one-in-four chance of getting burned doesn't seem like great odds on further analysis. Asked the specific problem, 44 percent named late delivery and 31 percent defective products. Other problems included getting a different version than what was ordered, misrepresentation of the product, delays in repair and difficulties in return. The most ominous problems were the least frequently cited: difficulty with unauthorized credit card charges (8 percent) and never receiving the product (7 percent).

Obviously, mail order has risks. But you can minimize them. Computer magazines don't put "sleazoid rip-off artist" logos in the ads of disreputable advertisers, but you can ask others who've bought by mail for referrals. Also, use credit cards instead of cash if possible. Federal law allows you to withhold payment on any credit card purchase of $50 or more if there's a dispute. You can't be forced to pay until the credit card company finishes its investigation. Likewise, you can't be held responsible for unauthorized charges. And card issuers are increasingly backing purchases with guarantees and warranties on top of what's offered by the seller.

One particularly comforting note: The *Macworld* survey found widespread satisfaction with customer support offered by mail-order vendors. Of mail-order buyers, 58 percent found support to be good or excellent, 13 percent fair and only 4 percent poor. One in four mail-order buyers didn't know how good the support was. (Either they never needed it, or maybe they never got their order.)

Other outlets are available more by chance than design. Check newspapers in your area for going-out-of-business sales, closings and auctions. If you know of a business that's closing and likely to have an inventory of computer hardware, don't wait for the ad. Check directly to find out how it plans to liquidate its computer equipment. You can also check classifieds for other sales of used hardware, which should be at a steep discount.

Used equipment, of course, comes with additional risks. You may not be able to tell what kind of use or abuse a computer got under a previous owner. Plan to at least take it for a test drive. Boot it and run your hardware. Ask if you can take it apart to look inside, checking for heavy accumulations of dust that signify poor maintenance.

Leasing: Weighing the Pros and Cons

Another way to reduce your initial investment is by leasing equipment. Computer stores, leasing companies and mail-order houses offer lease plans, so your options here are almost as varied as for buying hardware. It's difficult, however, to evaluate a lease by just looking at the numbers. For instance, a Mac IIsi with 5MB of RAM and 100MB of hard disk memory might cost $3,000 to $3,500 to buy—or it might cost $120 a month to lease, which seems like a good deal if you're strapped for cash. Buying on credit, however, is probably a better alternative. With a lease, you'll have paid an amount equal to the purchase price in a little more than two years with no equity to show for it. If you bought that same IIsi on credit at 18 percent interest, you'd have it paid off in two years for only about $150 a month.

But leasing can still be a good option under some circumstances, such as when you need a computer until you get enough cash to buy one. You also can use a lease to fill temporary needs, or start off with a low-end machine and move up to a high-end one.

Make sure you negotiate and read the lease carefully. What's the minimum term allowed? Can you upgrade without taking a bath? How long must you wait to upgrade? Can you get a lease-buy option? If so, how much would you ultimately end up paying for the equipment as opposed to buying it on credit? Remember to comparison shop for rent or lease rates as carefully as you would for an outright purchase. If you can, run some options for buying on credit through a spreadsheet or amortization program on a computer to see if the difference in payments is worth what you give up in accumulating equity.

Setting Up Shop on a Shoestring

Brian Bauer runs Digital Design in Somerville, Massachusetts, with one big client and one small outlay for equipment. His client, the mail-order catalog company North Country Corp. of Cambridge, Massachusetts, stayed with Bauer when the mail-order consulting company he worked for went out of business in 1985.

Bauer furnishes his toolbox in part by scouring the back pages of the newspaper—looking at classified ads, warehouse sales and auctions. "These things are going on all the time, and you can pick up incredible savings, especially on monitors and peripherals," he says. He bought his first add-on monitor, a full-page Radius that listed for $800, for $350 at a warehouse sale.

But his biggest equipment-buying break came because, he says, "I got a major break that would be very hard to duplicate." The source was a computer dealer in Cambridge that specialized in selling computer systems strictly for architects and designers. The dealer was long on attitude but short on customer service, Bauer says, and it shortly went out of business.

"They were having a going-out-of-business sale and all of the computer sales people were already gone," he says. "The only ones left were the bean counters." The accountants apparently cared more about getting the inventory out the door than making any profit on it. "I asked, 'How much is that box over there with the monitor in it?' expecting to hear $2,500. They said $700. I rummaged around and found the video control board for it that lists for $1,800 and they sold it to me for $800."

The going-out-of-business sale let Bauer upgrade in a hurry. The savings of $3,200 on his 19-inch color video system let him invest in a Mac IIfx with 8MB of RAM and a 185MB hard drive. The new system replaced Bauer's old Mac Plus, which he had acquired with a discount while he was a night student at Harvard.

"It was crazy economics," Bauer says, "but I saved enough on the video system at that going-out-of-business sale to buy the computer."

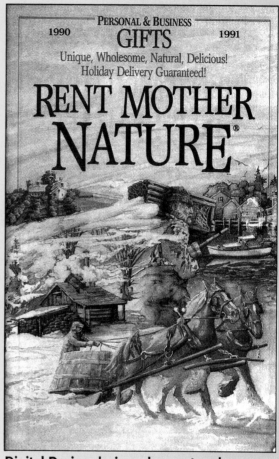

Digital Design designs, lays out and produces elaborate catalogs, like "Rent Mother Nature" (also shown on pages 15-16) for North Country Corp. of Cambridge, Massachusetts, entirely on the computer.

This inside spread of "Rent Mother Nature" was produced on the Mac IIfx Brian Bauer purchased with the money he saved by shopping at a going-out-of-business sale. (See page 16 for another inside spread of "Rent Mother Nature.")

Mastering Your Computer Tools

Learning to use software and hardware ultimately takes more time than buying it. Ideally, you became familiar with the equipment in an earlier life as employee or student. If not, your incarnation as a business operator could have some awfully bad karma at first.

Remember, what's cheapest in the beginning may not be so economical in the long run. Here are your options for mastering your computer tools in order of initial outlay:

■ *Option 1: Sit down and start pointing and clicking away.* This isn't necessarily as reckless as it sounds. You might as well see how far you can get this way before trying anything more involved or costly.

■ *Option 2: Read the manuals.* This is an option that works best for technical writers and people who think like technical writers. Even if you don't go this route at first, go back to your manuals after you've used the computer awhile. Then it all might start to make more sense, and you may pick up some valuable tips.

■ *Option 3: Read the computer magazines.* Ideally, you should have been doing this before you bought the equipment.

■ *Option 4: Buy books describing how to use your software.* These books go beyond the documentation and usually are much easier to use.

■ *Option 5: Join a user group.* You can choose one that meets in person or one that operates through on-line bulletin boards.

■ *Option 6: Take classes from the dealer.*

These classes may not cost much, and there's a reason for that: In many cases, they're more demonstrations than lessons. But if classes are one of your reasons for buying from a dealer, you might as well use them.

■ *Option 7: Buy videotape or audio/disk tutorials*. They're available from computer stores and through mail order. Since a tape training package can cost as much as a third or a half of what you paid for the software, it's not an investment to be taken lightly. Economies of scale make videos more sensible for larger operations.

■ *Option 8: Take "off the rack" classes offered by local computer training centers*. They don't come cheap, and they may not come with much insight into your special needs. But they are a good midrange-cost alternative for people who learn best in classrooms.

■ *Option 9: Buy interactive training programs for hard disk or CD-ROM*. These have several advantages. You don't have to look back and forth from the TV to the computer as you do with a VCR program. They're designed to respond to your input, show you your mistakes, and let you learn at your pace and on your schedule. The disadvantage is cost: Such programs run as much or more than off-the-rack classes.

■ *Option 10: Get custom training from a consultant who specializes in graphics applications*. This is by far the most expensive choice. But you may find the cost of up to $500 per student per day worthwhile if you're moving into very high-end areas such as color image editing and processing.

What You Need Besides the Computer

Don't think that you've stopped spending money when the computer system is bought. There's plenty more to outfitting your business.

■ *Desk*: The options are bewildering, and so are the prices for higher-end computer desks. Any desk of a comfortable height that will hold your equipment and give you enough room to work will do, including an old door on sawhorses. What else you need depends on your aesthetics and whether you plan to bring clients into the office for meetings.

■ *Chair*: Unlike the desk, scrimping here is a big mistake. You spend much of your life in that office chair; spend the $200 and up it takes for one that will make your life pleasant. Key factors to consider are durability, height adjustability, back support, arm support and ability to swivel, tilt and rock. The ideal chair is like a willow—yielding yet strong. (That's not to say a willow chair is ideal.)

■ *Filing system*: In case you haven't learned by now, the paperless office is a myth. Get a filing cabinet and make sure you have room to add more as your business grows.

■ *Bookshelves*: Like paper, books and manuals have a way of piling up. Plan on needing more capacity than you thought you wanted at first.

■ *Supplies*: Don't forget to take the rather staggering cost of laser paper and toner into account when setting up your office.

■ *Business checking and credit card accounts*: They're the only surefire way to keep your business and personal finances separate, especially for a home office.

■ *Phone lines*: Ideally you should have one for the phone and another for fax and/or modem. If your fax and modem traffic is slight, you can get by with one line. But you may lose some customers with busy signals. And you can't have call waiting on a fax/modem line, unless you can control rage when incoming calls knock out modem transmissions.

If you have a home office, the phone company expects you to pay for a business line. The advantages are that you can deduct 100 percent of a business line from your taxable income, and you can't take anything off for a residential line. Also, the business line usually gives you a one-line listing in the Yellow Pages and the opportunity to generate even more business with a display ad.

Staying Home vs. Going Out to Work

Low costs have made home offices prevalent in your business. If you have the overhead of an office, it's much harder to compete with home-

Slowly but Surely Plays Well in Peoria

When Kitty Ryan suffered a serious illness in 1986, she was forced to take a two-month leave of absence from her job at a Peoria, Illinois, ad agency. She recovered, but her career had a setback. She was demoted from media services director to researcher after she returned to work. Rather than get discouraged, she used the misfortune as motivation to start her own business. The divorced mother of a five-year-old son carefully laid the groundwork for her advertising and desktop publishing business over the next three years.

Ryan started freelance writing on the side while still employed at the agency. Her scant first-year earnings netted $1,800, which she invested in books, tape programs and a portable computer. She made $3,000 her second year and used that to buy a Macintosh SE computer. And she used her third-year earnings to buy a LaserWriter IINT printer.

With the equipment she needed to outfit her home office, Ryan decided to launch her business in April 1989. She sent marketing letters to three major companies in Peoria and lined up work from all three. Letting her college professors at Bradley University know she was starting her own business also led to referrals. "Other jobs just came from people I used to work with who knew somebody else who needed work," she says. And DeskTop Ink was born.

Her three-year preparation also paid off with a portfolio bulging with a variety of work samples, Ryan says. "I could have gotten a ton of nonprofit work when I started out, but I couldn't take it because it didn't pay much, or anything at all," Ryan says. "I would have had a giant portfolio, but no money. As it was, my portfolio was plenty big enough before I quit my job, and I didn't need any more brochures or articles with my name on them."

Preparation has been one of Ryan's hallmarks. She has bachelor's degrees in speech communications and journalism, which followed earlier course work that included much of what she would need for a graphic arts degree.

"I had a lot of background that most people wouldn't get, plus experience following projects through production from start to finish," Ryan says. That experience helped her get the projects she likes most: big ones for which clients have a rough idea of what they want but need someone to develop all aspects, from concept to copywriting to design and production.

"I want those jobs that go into the thousands rather than mess with the $20 to $60 jobs here and there," Ryan says. She has done plenty of those small jobs, particularly when she started out. But her copywriting experience helped her land bigger ones by diversifying her services. "Typesetting and layout are the parts of what I offer that people seem to understand the most," Ryan says. "I had to explain to people that I was also a writer and could help get them through the whole thing."

On the equipment front, Ryan found layout duties called for a RasterOps two-page monitor and SE accelerator board, bought with profits from her first year of business. She was shortly making more money working for herself than she did at the agency, and her profits allowed her to buy a new home three times bigger than her previous one with a spare 10-by-14-foot bedroom for her business.

One thing her preparation couldn't provide, however, was a health plan. Ultimately, lack of coverage forced Ryan to take a copywriting job in 1991 with a major client who had been asking her to become an employee. But Ryan still works from her home, and she still operates her own copywriting/design business as a sideline. In a way, it's like having one big client, she says. "Before, since I had a home office and my own business, it felt like I was working the entire day," she says. "Now, I'm done at 5:00, and I'm kind of liking that."

based colleagues on price. You either have to settle for being less profitable, hope your higher visibility in an outside office improves the volume and quality of your work, or charge more and hope customers will be willing to pay it.

Still, there are pros and cons to working at home. The hectic deadlines and sometimes long hours that go with desktop design and publishing lend themselves to a home office. If you have to pull an all-nighter to get the job out the door, it's a little less stressful from the confines of your own home. Balancing these advantages are the numerous distractions home offers: kids, pets, food, hobbies and electronic entertainment galore. And the workday can get stretched from the normal 9:00-to-5:00 to something more like 7:00 A.M. to midnight, with a series of scattered breaks.

Image was once a factor weighing against working from home. But the image problem is diminishing as home offices become more common. The number of self-employed people working at home reached 11.8 million nationwide in 1991, up 5.4 percent from just a year earlier, according to Link Resources Corp., a research consulting firm. Even if the image of a home office is improving, many desktop designers and publishers are uncomfortable receiving clients in their homes. That can necessitate extra travel time going to the client's office or entertaining clients at lunch — and picking up the tab.

Location is another problem. Your home in a bedroom community may not be convenient to business customers — requiring you to make long trips or forego much of your potential market. Your home office is also less likely to be near key vendors, such as service bureaus and printers.

And the home office can severely crimp expansion plans. Hiring employees to work in your home or bringing contractors to work there opens a legal can of worms — particularly with zoning issues. Residential zoning in many areas permits home-based professional businesses, provided they don't operate as storefronts and don't have employees. Whatever your zoning regulations may — or may not — allow, cooperating with neighbors is the key. If they don't complain, the authorities aren't

likely to come around beating the bushes for desktop designers and publishers. If you were operating a machine shop in your spare bedroom, the noise might get on the neighbors' nerves. Fortunately, yours is a pretty unobtrusive business. But hanging out a shingle or having a heavy flow of customers, contractors or employees through your house could aggravate the neighbors.

Tips for Finding Office Space

If you started business in a home office, you may eventually decide an outside office or studio is best as your business grows. When looking for commercial space, consider the following:

- *Location.* How close are your service bureaus and printers? Are you near many potential clients? If not, are you at least convenient to major highways that will get you there faster? Street visibility is a minor consideration for your business, since you probably won't get a lot of walk-in traffic and you may have to pay more for highly accessible spots. But will it be easy to tell people how to find you?

- *Appearance.* If professional image is your reason for wanting an outside office, don't blow it by renting space in a run-down building. That doesn't mean you have to rent new, top-notch office space; there are plenty of well-maintained older buildings.

- *Classification.* Building owners classify most office space three ways. Class A is newer space in choice locations with top amenities, such as modern heating and air conditioning. Class A buildings have large floorplates and want big companies to fill them. Class B space is either older Class A property that's slipping in terms of maintenance, or top-notch property in less convenient locations. Most suburban or small-town office space, for instance, no matter how new or good, is really Class B because it's not downtown. Class C space could be where the neighborhood or the building leaves a lot to be desired — or it could just be a small building without parking or other amenities but otherwise well maintained and attractive. If it's the latter, Class C can be a good value.

- *Character.* Older renovated buildings, either Class B or Class C, can have lots of character, with all the exposed brick and wood. Design studios of all types seem to thrive in such spaces. Modern steel-and-glass skyscrapers and sprawling suburban officeplexes sometimes lack soul; it seems a little harder to work up creative energy in one of them.

■ *On-site services.* Some office buildings that cater to small businesses offer on-site secretarial, answering and other services that can give you a lot of bang for the rental buck. Such complexes also have lots of potential customers for your work and often a congenial atmosphere that makes networking easy.

■ *Subleasing.* Two trends affecting commercial real estate make subleasing increasingly possible. First, the building boom of the eighties created a buyer's market in Class A space in most central business districts. Lease rates didn't come down officially, but building owners threw in mammoth "incentives," amounting to years of free rent for many companies. But after a few years, the companies had to start paying and suddenly realized they didn't really need all that space. Also, corporate downsizing has peeled layers of management away at many companies, leaving them with empty office space. You may be able to get a good rate on a sublease. And because the employees left behind in a corporate restructuring are often overburdened, they may be eager to hand some of their work to you.

Chapter Two

Markets for Your Services

Computers haven't exactly made graphic design an off-the-shelf commodity where one product's as good as the next. But they have leveled the playing field some, allowing thousands of competitors in all facets of the market. Your artistic ability and technical expertise will set you apart from millions of other computer owners, but it still is the computer that makes your skill work better, faster and cheaper than that of conventional artists.

Whether you're a highly trained graphic artist or a neophyte, there are several ways to try your hand in desktop design and publishing. Here are some issues to consider as you develop your specialty and your market niches.

Finding Your Specialties

Discovering the most productive way to make money with your desktop computer means assessing your skills and interests to see where you fit. Here are the major areas of design services, and how your computer influences your place in these areas.

Design and Layout

You can design everything from postcards to three-dimensional product design on computers. Though they make the job easier, they're no substitute for a specialized education in graphic arts or industrial design. Many designers become computer users, but it's far more difficult for computer users to become designers without additional training.

One of the biggest strengths of desktop design and publishing has been in the area of page layout. Never has experimentation been easier. The effect of computers on page layouts may have been bigger than that of cold type and the offset press. Just compare a few newspapers and magazines from fifteen years ago to today's. For ad layouts, fliers and posters, bona fide designers have a definite edge. But a nonartist with a bent for reader-friendly design can do quite well in publication layout.

Production

This is the area where desktop computers have had the most sweeping effect. Production is the area most open to those with little or no formal

design training, and it can be a doorway to more highly skilled areas. Since the computer combines layout, typesetting and paste-up functions into one job, it gives production artists a chance to round out and upgrade their skills.

High-end jobs still need imagesetting for the output, but the input, layout and placement of elements can be done on a desktop computer, and the creation of proofs can be done with a laser printer. Laser printers still don't reliably approach the resolution of imagesetting equipment. That keeps typesetting machines and type houses in business. But for lower-end jobs, conventional typesetting is virtually a thing of the past. Besides replacing conventional typesetting, desktop computers provide options typesetting equipment never did. Designers can use their computers to create or at least modify typefaces for specialized jobs. Others have developed proprietary typefaces, turning their studios into electronic type foundries.

The high-end of the production front is still the province of relatively few highly skilled graphics computer operators. With the revolution in desktop color capabilities of the nineties, color image editing, photo processing and photo stripping can be easily handled on computers. Technology now lets graphics computer systems go straight from file to film, or file to plate.

The highly skilled work and the expensive equipment put in-house color pre-press work out of reach for most desktop publishers. But

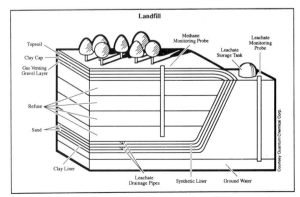

Technical illustration is one area where desktop computers excel, offering the benefits of previously impossible special effects and time savings over conventional methods.

as with other aspects of desktop design and publishing, the equipment should become more accessible and affordable.

Graphics and Illustration

Graphic effects that would have been impossible or impractical by conventional means have become the norm, thanks to computers. The explosion of information graphics started by *USA Today* and spread to virtually every newspaper in the country is but one example. For logos, letterheads, forms and other aspects of corporate identity graphics, computers make perfecting the final product much easier and faster. The inspiration works as well with or without a computer, but the computer wins hands down in the execution department.

Yet there are plenty of areas the computer has yet to master. Freehand illustration, for instance, is still easier and better with free hand than FreeHand.

Publishing and Copywriting

A desktop computer system won't make you a publisher, but it can make things a whole lot easier. Shrinking the composing room and the editorial office into a box on your desk makes putting out any publication considerably cheaper. Whether you develop your own publications or produce them for others, this is one of your biggest advantages as a desktop publisher.

Design-oriented desktop publishers probably don't get as many requests for copywriting as copywriters get requests for desktop publishing. But the more services you can offer, the more indispensable and economical you become for your clients, and the more you can make on each job. If you can't be a copywriter, it's probably a good idea to at least know one or two. In many cases, clients turn to you for jobs that an ad agency, with its pool of designers and writers, would handle. One reason they'll turn to you is that they're more likely to understand the need for design than the need for copywriting. Another is that you're much cheaper than an agency. But you can be nearly as good as one by forging a long-term relationship with a copywriter or pool of copywriters. Then you can form a team for projects that

---

Computer vs. Traditional Methods

Desktop design and publishing can beat traditional methods in a number of areas:

- Publication design
- Publication layout
- Advertising layout
- Typesetting
- Preparation of camera-ready mechanicals
- Color image editing
- Photo editing
- Information graphics
- Technical illustrations
- Photo stripping
- Keylining
- Color separations

---

need both services, and you can develop a two-way network of client referrals.

Freelancing for Designers vs. Other Clients

One of the largest markets for desktop designers and publishers is other graphic artists. You can offer small- and medium-size design studios access to the equipment and experience without the overhead and training headaches. If nothing else, you can give design studios a quicker and cheaper way to set type. They can bring you in during peak work loads without having to keep you on the payroll during lean times.

Freelancing for designers has lots of benefits for you, too. It gives you access to jobs and clients you'd have trouble landing on your own. The design studio bears the burden of marketing, billing and, in some cases, collecting. Provided the studio pays you on time, that spares you the dirty work of chasing down delinquent accounts. But freelancing also has disadvantages. If you rely on design studios for all of your work, you have no control over your cash flow or destiny. Their responsibility is to make money for themselves, not to keep you well fed

Freelancing for Designers

When Joel Williams started his desktop design and publishing business in 1988, he had a background in newspaper design, photo editing and information graphics. But he had no formal training in graphic design. Working for designers, however, has been the mainstay of his business from the beginning, making up 60 percent of Cincinnati-based Chelsea Design's work. After years of experience and some graphic design classes, Williams has become a designer in his own right, working largely for other designers.

"I work directly with designers on large typesetting projects, providing them services they could get through more traditional outlets but at a much better rate," Williams says. "I can provide not just typesetting, but everything in position and high-quality comps." Williams offers designers access to Mac technology without having to buy the equipment, hire and train staff, or climb the learning curve.

Early on, finding the best formula to decide what he and his clients would handle was sometimes a problem, he says. Now, he finds most projects have settled into a pattern. For a typical project, such as a newsletter or brochure, Williams's client meets with his or her client, develops the concept, makes some rough sketches of the initial design and specs type. Then Williams gets the sketches, type specs and a disk with the copy on it.

"At that point, I'm operating somewhat as a traditional typesetter would, except that I'm also interpreting the rough sketches and putting everything in position, incorporating the paste-up into the process as well," he says.

Later, Williams works with the designer to "hammer out a lot of the intricacies of the design," he says. "That's where it becomes more than just a typesetting job, because the designers I work with respect my opinion and my background, so we blend our experience to come up with the best ideas."

Williams and the designer then go back to the client with black-and-white comps from Williams's LaserWriter IINT or color comps from a service bureau. Usually the client asks for changes that result in one or two revised comps. Then Williams works with the service bureau to get final Linotronic output.

For some color jobs, the designer marks up the color separations needed on overlays, and Williams does color breaks on the Mac for later Linotronic color separations at the service bureau. He uses a monochrome monitor, so the color laser output is his first chance to see the color, other than envisioning it with his PMS color wheel. For more intricate color jobs, Williams relies on the printer for separations. "Even though I'm billing the designer for those services and paying the type vendor for the final mechanical, I'm still saving everybody a lot of money in the long run because we're just editing laser output, not galleys from the typesetter," he says.

Since starting business, Williams has taken a graphic design course at the University of Cincinnati to expand his knowledge of conventional design. It wasn't easy to get into the highly competitive program, but the professor thought it would be good for design students to interact with a professional desktop designer and publisher. While the students were a little reluctant to accept an electronic designer with little formal background into their midst, Williams felt he benefited. "I felt like I really didn't have the background I needed, and I wanted to develop my skills in other media to enhance the Macintosh work," he says. "If you're totally dependent on the Macintosh, it can be a real dead end, because there are a lot of things that still have to be done by conventional means."

and happy. If they don't attract new business, you'll be the first to suffer.

The designer also controls the kind of work you do and how it's created. And the studio gets a cut of your potential profit. You might make more money by developing your own client base than by working through studios, because you could get what you're making plus at least part of the markup a studio charges.

Those things considered, freelancing for other designers is still an important market. Few other industries have as great a need for your work. And being a contractor for a studio can give you a chance to build skills and a portfolio to help you land clients on your own later.

When Debbie Anagnost started her business in San Francisco, she worked exclusively for three local studios. She didn't have her own equipment, so freelancing was really her only option. But the work she got let her save to buy a Macintosh IIsi and all the software she needed. It also gave her time to develop a promotional piece to use when she began seeking work on her own.

"The only disadvantage," she says, "is that you're not really working for yourself. It's not your own work, because it's for somebody else."

Collaborating With Other Professionals

Like freelancing for studios, collaborating with other communications professionals creates a synergy that lets you do more and better business. Your collaboration can take many forms, such as:

- A partnership or joint venture with someone whose skills complement your own, thereby helping you both attract more clients.
- An informal network bound by mutual referrals.
- A consortium, with administrative marketing staff, supported by member professionals.
- A private company that markets the services of selected communications professionals, either as employees or independent contractors.

The first two options are less involved, so they're easier to accomplish. The latter two, however, may have more potential. They can form teams on a per-project basis, giving clients the depth of a large agency without charging them for all the overhead.

Types of professionals you may want to work with are:

- Copywriters
- Editors
- Illustrators
- Photographers
- Market research specialists
- Advertising executives
- Audio/video specialists
- Animators
- Public relations specialists
- Technical writers
- Scriptwriters

Market Niches: Where You Fit

Being a desktop designer and publisher gives you the technology and the know-how to do all kinds of work—from exquisitely designed posters to more mundane but no less essential price lists. You may start business with a very narrow idea of which kinds of services you'll offer and which kinds of media you'll use. But there's a world of opportunity you may not have considered. What follows is a trip through the many market areas where you and your computer can fit.

Collateral Materials

This wide-ranging category includes brochures, fliers, product data sheets, booklets, posters and a variety of "leave-behinds" used to promote companies, their products or individuals. These materials may support a company's ad or public relations campaign, but they're separate from it, and often handled by different people. The company may not want to foot the bill for an agency to handle the work or hire full-time employees to handle occasional needs, so collateral materials are a way for you to get a foot in the door.

Pros: Collateral materials offer plenty of creative potential and money. For large companies

Cooperating to Get and Keep Accounts

George Fiala's desktop design and publishing business is so diversified, you might not think he'd want much more diversity. His Brooklyn-based Select Mail, Inc. handles design and typesetting for a variety of promotional materials, from display ads to letterhead. He also has a brisk résumé service business. And his mailing services include mailing-list sales and management, label printing, and mailing out mail. But Fiala broadens his approach further as a member of Brooklyn Communication Arts Professionals, whose meetings give him a chance to network with other professionals.

"The group publishes a directory, and some people think that's going to bring them a lot of business," Fiala says. "It does bring some, but the real value is in being part of the group, meeting people in your line of work and making connections."

For instance, Fiala works on newsletters and other projects with a marketing communications specialist and an illustrator. The three also pooled their efforts on a joint mailing to attract new clients. Fiala handled the design, typography and production of mechanicals for the postcard mailer. He also provided a 3,000-name mailing list, printed mailing labels and paid for postage. The marketing specialist paid for the printing and wrote copy for the back of the card, which carried her business's name as the contact. And the illustrator created a humorous cartoon to anchor the piece. The mailing generated for the participants lots of interest and one major client, the Brooklyn Private Industry Council, which administers a federal job-training and placement program for youth.

Fiala feels that collaborating with other professionals helps him give clients more than he could provide on his own. That, in turn, helps him land clients he never could otherwise. For the Private Industry Council, the team could provide top-notch advice on how the client could reach its target market: Brooklyn-area employers. Then the marketing company, the illustrator and Fiala worked together to produce copy, illustrations

and layouts for a brochure mailing. The Private Industry Council got the services an ad agency could provide at well under half the price, Fiala says.

Besides collaborating with graphic artists and copywriters, Fiala also finds cooperating with printers fruitful. While many printers have in-house desktop design and publishing operations, many more don't. Working closely with such printers brings referrals and the chance for extra income by selling clients printing as part of the job.

"You might charge someone $75 for producing something," he says, "and then make another $75 just by brokering the printing."

Are things too quiet at YOUR office?

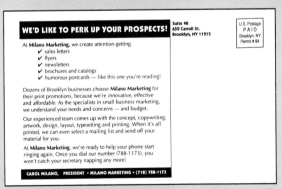

George Fiala of Select Mail, Inc. collaborated with an illustrator and a marketing specialist to produce and distribute this mailer. Milano Marketing served as the clearinghouse for all jobs that resulted from this collaboration. The piece landed them a job with the Private Industry Council, which works with local employers to develop job training programs.

Producing sales flyers for home builders, like this one produced by Corporate Publishing, Inc. of Cincinnati, can provide plenty of repeat business.

The Griffin House

The Griffin, a detached condominium home, designed for those who desire one-floor living. Two bedrooms, a solarium (or 3rd bedroom), great room and eat-in kitchen are all part of a true ranch plan which maximizes the accessibility of all rooms. The great room is highlighted by vaulted ceiling and woodburning fireplace. Master bedroom opens onto a large wood deck, as does the solarium. The master bath offers a laundry, walk-in closet, double bowl vanity and skylight. Each homesite backs onto a private wooded setting. The full basement and attached two-car garage are additional features that make this the best value in condominium living in the Greater Cincinnati area.

The Griffin House

Hyde Park Associates
DEVELOPERS & BUILDERS

Model Home Office: 474-5670

Dunne
& Associates.

with ever-changing products, collateral materials are a market that keeps growing. Even small and midsize companies may have a surprisingly large array of collateral materials. That's because they cost much less than other promotional strategies, such as advertising. Collateral materials are somewhat recession-resistant, because in hard times companies may adjust their promotional campaigns to include more collateral materials and fewer higher-priced options.
Cons: Collateral materials don't have any built-in obsolescence or time value like newsletters, magazines or annual reports. Therefore, there's no guarantee of repeat business.
Untapped opportunities: For every piece of collateral material you see, you can probably think of another product or company that could use some. How many real estate agents, for instance, keep detailed fliers on homes they list as leave-behinds for potential buyers or to send out of town for corporate transfers? If you could convince just a handful of agents of the value of using such materials, you could have a substantial market.

Annual Reports
This staple of corporate America may seem unapproachable for an independent desktop designer and publisher, but it's not. Because annual reports are a crucial promotional piece used to lure investors, customers and employees alike, most Fortune 500 companies handle them in-house or contract with top ad agencies or annual report specialty firms. But that doesn't mean there's no place for you in this market.

The service you provide—the ability to expertly combine text and graphics—is exactly what makes annual reports. Cracking the market with a Fortune 500 company may be tough, but thousands of smaller companies with public shareholders also issue annual reports. That doesn't even count the thousands of annual reports published each year by entities not required to do so by the Securities and Exchange Commission: charitable and other nonprofit organizations, public and private schools, colleges and more. These organizations are much more approachable, and much more likely not to have the staff to handle the duties in-house.

Specialized experience in financial documents and corporate communications is a big plus for breaking into this market. If you don't have it, you may benefit by linking up with a copywriter who does. The client usually provides copy, but she or he may want help in punching it up. More important, however, is your ability to turn this collection of balance sheets and corporate-speak into something visually enticing. If the words can't captivate the reader—and they probably won't—the design may have to.
Pros: Annual reports are a lock for repeat business if you do the job well. Because they're a big project that only comes around once a year, corporations and organizations almost always need help with some part of them. These are among the highest-profile and highest-paying jobs available. A single annual report can be a substantial account you can depend on at the same time every year. And by breaking the billing into chunks, you also can manage a fairly smooth cash flow.
Cons: An annual report is a heavy task that can weigh down a small operation. It may require your undivided attention for months. Because it's crucial, the annual report gets intense scrutiny from all areas of management. You may need approvals from a CEO and numerous division heads, all of whom will be jockeying to make sure they're portrayed in the best possible light. As a result, the report can be a political football, with a lot of grief and aggravation. An annual report also can be a cash flow headache if you don't structure the contract to get a substantial portion of your payment up front. Don't wait months to get paid for a project this big.
Untapped opportunities: Corporations whose stock is sold to the public are required by federal law to publish annual reports. But nonprofit organizations can use annual reports as a fundraising vehicle or to maintain supporter trust—and you might be the one to convince them of such. Any smaller company that handles the annual report in-house could be approached about using an outside vendor; it simply makes sense for such a seasonal need. And while many small companies are private concerns that don't have to publish annual reports, they can still use them to impress and

Employee newsletters, like this one produced by Sharon Baldwin Sittner for Viox Services Inc. of Cincinnati, can mean steady business. Being able to provide clients with both design and editorial service can be a big plus in getting accounts and maximizing profits from each job.

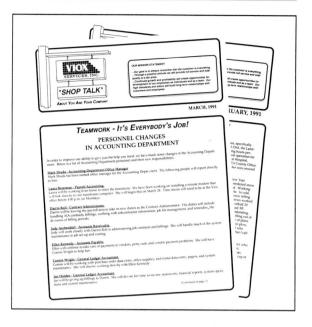

Toria Latnie - Accounting Clerk.
Toria will be helping everyone in the Accounting Department with special projects. She will also help with the telephones and typing.

Wendy Glen - Receptionist.
Wendy will continue as our receptionist but look forward to her moving out of the house and into the main building reception area in the near future.

We are confident these changes will improve our service to you.
If you have any questions or problems, just give us a call!

GOOD NEWS AND BAD NEWS

Brendon McCracken of our Painting Division had some good news and some bad news to share with us.

The bad news was that his house was broken into and robbed.

But the good news that Brendon wanted to share was that he was very pleased with the way the insurance company handled his problem. The company? Frederick Rauh, through our company payroll deductions!

WAY TO GO!

Peggy Carson, SWTC, wrote to thank:

Steeve Poole
Pat Grogan
Tom Fox
Jack Yost, Sr.
Tim Morrissey &
the cabinet shop

for their excellent planning, workmanship, and for reaching the targeted completion date on the sensory testing facility in the C Building at Sharon Woods.

Way to go, guys!

G.C. DIVISION AWARDED JOB

Congratulations to the G.C. Division!

They have been awarded all interior finishes for buildings #58 and #71 at P&G's St. Bernard Plant. They will be working with Fluor Daniels, the construction management firm, on this large-scale project.

We are trying to recycle all white office paper and computer paper. This includes letterhead, bond paper, copier paper, adding machine tapes, etc.

The following items should <u>not</u> be included:

Envelopes
Post-It Notes
Colored Paper
Gum Wrappers

Thanks for your help!

ABC CODE OF ETHICS

Following is a code of ethics developed by the Associated Builders and Contractors. As a member of ABC, we endorse and subscribe to each of the following commitments.

- To maintain a standard of performance consistent with the owner's best interest.

- To quote only realistic prices and completion dates and performance accordingly.

- To fully cooperate with the architect and other agents of the owner toward fulfillment of the contract undertaken.

- To solicit and accept bids and/or quotations only from firms with whom we are willing to do business.

- To make all payments promptly within the terms of the contract.

- To observe and foster the highest standards of safety and working conditions for employees.

- To establish fair wage schedules for employees commensurate with their ability and their industry.

- To actively participate in the training of skilled tradespersons for the future welfare of the construction industry.

COMMITMENT

AIR TRAVEL - EXTRA SECURITY PRECAUTIONS

Prestige Travel, Inc. tells us that the major airlines have instituted the following guidelines and rules to ensure greater security and safety.

Domestic Air Travel:
+ No curb side baggage check-in.
+ No ticket/remote office check-in.
+ Only ticketed passengers are allowed past security check points.
+ To expedite check-in, place objects with batteries or wires in carry-on luggage.
+ "Rule of Thumb" = arrive 90 minutes prior to flight departure; however, 2 hours is suggested during peak periods.
+ All check-in luggage will be electronically screened and safeguarded from the moment it is checked until retrieved by the passenger.

International Air Travel:
+ Extra security at gateway airports.
+ Same rules as domestic flights.
+ Check with travel agent regarding transportation of electronic devices as international carriers vary with respect to rules and restrictions.
+ Minimum check-in is 2 hrs. prior to departure.
+ Ask for the travel advisory list issued by the State Department or call (202) 647-5225 to hear the full text of an advisory.

DON'T MISS OUT!

Don't miss out on your opportunity to enjoy a hearty made-to-order breakfast and a chance to air your thoughts, concerns, and ideas about the company with Ray and John Viox.

To enter the monthly drawing for "Breakfast With The Bosses," just call Mikie Shorten at the office.

Breakfasts are normally held on the fourth Monday of the month at 7:30 a.m. in the main office.

EMPLOYEES OF THE MONTH

Jan Holden - Accounting
Jan currently handles all billings plus general ledger accounting and is learning the IBM 36 system operation. She is a part-time worker, but puts in extra hours each week to make certain her job is complete and accurate. Jan is extremely pleasant to work with, and she takes pride in her work.

Her new duties will include more specific general ledger accounting and system operations.

Dan Ferguson - Landscape Division
Dan has worked on snow removal 20 plus hours in one day on three or four occasions just this year. He is always the first person in to work, no matter what time of day or night we might need him or what the weather conditions might be.

We really appreciate Dan's hard work and dedication.

JANITORIAL EMPLOYEE OF THE MONTH

Congratulations, Tracy McCollum!

You've been named Employee of the Month for the Janitorial Division. Thanks for your hard work and dedication!

GREAT CUSTOMER SERVICE

F. A. Zakrajsek, SWTC, wrote to express his appreciation for the fine work and support provided by Jim Pike and Ron Hagemann during a recent office move.

Mr. Zakrajsek pointed out that they both appeared on time and were "very cooperative in providing for our every need. Our request for changes in our original plans were met with an equally cooperative effort."

A big thanks to Jim and Ron.

EMPLOYEE ANNIVERSARY

Congratulations to Jerry Gertz, who will celebrate his 10-year anniversary with Viox on March 30. Here's wishing you 10 more and then some, Jerry!

QUALITY

keep in touch with their clients and to bring employees up to date on company progress. You might be able to sell them on this point if your portfolio contains annual reports that can deliver in those areas.

Newsletters

Everyone from accountants to dry cleaners can use newsletters as a way to keep their names in front of clients. Newsletters can be cost-effective, and they're one of the most appropriate media for any business whose service is knowledge-based, because there's no better way to take on an air of authority. The fact that so many newsletters are competing for attention means that people need your help more than ever to make theirs stand out.

Employee newsletters range from glossy four-color magazines to mimeographed sheets. But they all fulfill the same need for management to inform, or at least project an image to, their employees. Mom-and-Pop operations do this directly, when Mom and Pop talk with the hired hands. It's the larger companies that need to communicate more formally.

There are two main types of newsletters:

■ *External.* These include a variety of promotional newsletters published by a wide range of businesses. They range from thinly veiled advertising fliers to newsletters that contain a mix of useful information and subtle propaganda. Editorial and design are equally important functions, and many clients will be receptive to anyone who can take the whole chore off their hands. So it may pay to network with a copywriter on newsletter jobs.

■ *Internal.* These are employee publications. Though some companies use their employee newsletters as promotional tools with outside vendors and clients, they usually stay in-house. Most companies don't devote the resources or the staff to produce high-quality employee publications. Doing the house organ may be crammed into the job description of someone who has little interest, inclination or time to put it out. That's where you come in. You can provide the expertise to take this chore through the production process and make it look professional.

Pros: Newsletters can be the ultimate in steady work. Once you've established an account, you can depend on the work monthly, quarterly—however often it's published. Each newsletter, even a basic two-pager, is a substantial job.

Cons: Newsletters only are a reliable source of business if the company is committed to sticking with them. They could be a low priority for the business, in which case it could be hard to get the information you need to put the newsletter out, much less keep future ones coming. The result could be a time crunch, an interruption in your other projects, or even a missed issue or two. Another con: Increasing clutter caused by the explosion of external newsletters may discourage prospective clients.

Untapped opportunities: Any business, particularly professional businesses such as accounting, financial planning and consulting, is missing the boat by not using a newsletter to communicate with clients. You might be able to offer such a business a relatively pain-free alternative. Large corporations may have more than one internal newsletter: one going to management, one to hourly workers, and one to retirees, for example. Some professional organizations offer members "generic" newsletters that they can personalize by adding a nameplate; these boilerplate jobs may be cheap, but it's not hard to spot them. You can offer businesses a way to improve these newsletters' design and add more information of their own. Or you can use your own generic format and personalize it for professionals in different industries. Another alternative is creating newsletter templates and selling them to clients on disk. You can do a better job than off-the-rack versions already available, because your templates will be better designed and have more industry-specific features. But you still give cost-conscious clients a cheaper alternative than hiring a designer or contracting a design firm. You won't make as much money as you would servicing that account yourself month after month, but you will open doors to more potential clients.

Many companies big enough to use employee publications don't. If you have a track record of producing good house organs, try to sell them on one. It may be a hard sell, because an em-

Good News, Bad News in Newsletters

Thom Hartmann was sold on newsletters long before he sold anyone else on them. He had owned several businesses in the seventies and eighties, including an ad agency. And he used newsletters to promote each one. For one organization, a nonprofit agency in Atlanta to care for abused children, a newsletter was Hartmann's primary fundraising vehicle. But when he went to Germany to work for the group's parent organization, he found out how hard it was to find someone else to publish his newsletter well and economically. An ad agency would do a good job but quoted him $2,000 a page. A printer wanted only $50 a page, but he didn't think the work would meet his expectations. "I felt there was a business opportunity for someone who could provide a good quality product at a price somewhere between those two extremes," he says. "So, when I came back from Europe, I started the business."

The business is The Newsletter Factory Inc., started in 1987 as a two-person operation in Marietta, Georgia, handling all aspects of newsletter production for clients. In four years, the company grew into a fifteen-employee operation with a national sales force, Fortune 1000 clients, and a bustling sideline business giving one hundred seminars a year on newsletter production for corporations.

The most Hartmann charges is $1,500 a page, only 75 percent of the quote he got from the ad agency. For that rate, his clients get everything from conceptual development to complete editorial, design and production services. To do design and production alone, he charges $200-$250 per page. "We have several levels of service," he says. "We can do the design and lay down the type and produce the mechanicals. Or we can edit their work. We can rewrite stories from magazines and newspapers for their newsletters. Or we can do it all from scratch."

Though many customers only want help with the design, Hartmann feels The Newsletter Factory's range of services gives it a competitive edge. The Newsletter Factory tries to create "newsy" newsletters two ways. Editorially, he uses news summaries or news stories on the front page, mixed with feature stories elsewhere, to attract reader interest. Straightforward designs like those for *Time* or *Newsweek*—with ruled columns, crisp typography and perfectly cropped photos—work best, he says.

The external newsletter market is driven by increased use for client communication, to keep a company's name in front of current or prospective clients. Newsletters are more likely to get passed through a client's office and convey a complex message than other forms of print media, Hartmann says. The clutter caused by the proliferation of external newsletters, however, is a problem—but it's one he thinks drives clients his way in an effort to make their newsletters rise above the rest.

Today, Hartmann can afford sales reps, billboards, radio spots and sponsorship of public TV shows. But his chief marketing vehicle, not surprisingly, is a newsletter, called *Newsletter Communications*. It's an outlet he's used from the outset of his business. "We've found the most effective tool has been our own newsletter," he says. "It tends to be synergistic. People may have heard our radio ads for three months, but when they get the newsletter, that pushes them over the edge and makes them call."

NEWSLETTER
Communications™

WRITING TIPS INSIDE!

NEWS & INFORMATION
TO HELP PROFESSIONALS
USE NEWSLETTERS
FOR CORPORATE
COMMUNICATIONS

Newsletters Can Rescue Your Marketing Budget While Increasing Sales!

BY THOMAS HARTMANN

Tight financial times are causing many companies to seek ways to save money without sacrificing the effectiveness of their marketing programs. They're looking hard at advertising costs, and often deciding to cut back.

An economic downturn, however, is often the worst time to consider cutting back on marketing efforts. It slows down sales and causes customer loyalty to disintegrate, thus creating a downward spiral that simply feeds on itself.

So what's a company to do when it has to cut back on advertising expenses, but still wants to maintain customer contact, get out its advertising message, and prospect for new business? A newsletter!

Newsletters offer many businesses the most cost-effective marketing tools available.

- **Newsletters have high credibility.** Most people, when reading an advertisement or flyer, have a little voice in the back of their heads saying, "This is an advertisement. People lie in advertisements. Don't believe this."

Properly designed newsletters, however, are viewed not as an advertisement, but instead as news. People read them with "suspended disbelief," assuming that the information is "news" and not "hype." Offering industry news and presenting information that's useful to clients (how-to stories are a good example) are two excellent methods for building such credibility.

- **Newsletters are inexpensive compared to other forms of advertising.** They're generally self-mailers, not requiring the cost of an envelope. They usually don't require expensive printing to look good.

Continued on page 2

Efficient Proofing Means Checking the Obvious...Again and Again

BY G.W. HALL

You'll virtually eliminate mistakes from your newsletter if you thoroughly re-check *all* information at *every stage* of the production process.

A proper proofing system begins with a complete examination of text before the design process ever gets under way. At The Newsletter Factory®, for example, mistakes are detected by assigning at least two experienced proofreaders to check each article before our designers begin layout. If you don't have that option, read the material slowly and carefully, or have a detail-oriented co-worker do it for you. And always pay especially close attention if you wrote the article yourself—your brain will gloss over errors because it knows what you *meant* to say.

Once your newsletter enters design, conscientiously re-examine every article during each design proof, again using extreme care if you've made changes. At The Newsletter Factory®, for example, our proofers confirm that all changes were made properly and no accidental errors occurred before

Continued on page 4

JHWH

Practicing what it preaches, The Newsletter Factory Inc. in Atlanta uses *Newsletter Communications*, its own external newsletter, as its primary marketing tool.

ployee publication is not a revenue-generator. But you can try to sell them on benefits such as improved morale and increased productivity. Give concrete examples of the benefits from other companies you've worked with. One approach is to develop a generic format or template that can be customized easily as a prototype and selling tool for different companies.

Marketing Materials

This is another vast category, which includes direct-mail packages and display advertising design. The dollars spent on direct mail or print advertising each year dwarfs that spent on newsletters or collateral material. Although much of the market is controlled by ad agencies, you can crack this market in many ways— particularly direct mail.

Most larger companies have in-house staff to handle the direct-mail work load. But smaller companies and retailers could probably use your help, if they knew you were available. To take full advantage of this market, you must provide clients with a team that can handle the whole job, including copywriting, design and pre-press production. You'll also need to contract for printing and mailing.

Display advertising design is a little harder market to crack. Ad agencies or publications handle most of this work in-house. But you may be able to contract with smaller players in either of these areas as a backup to handle peak work loads during the holiday season. And smaller community publications may rely completely on outside vendors.

Pros: Businesses that don't use some form of direct mail are the exception rather than the rule. Even if you limit yourself to small retailers and other businesses in your neighborhood or community, you can probably generate a significant amount of business. Direct mail and display advertising alike let you use your design creativity to the max. And these media are perfect for desktop designers and publishers, who can keep client projects on disk to easily revise product information, seasonal angles, etc.

Cons: Unlike newsletters and other periodicals, there's no guarantee direct mailers will keep needing your services month after month. You'll need to develop a large client base to

Small local retailers seldom have the resources to produce display ads in-house. Independent designers offer them the ability to have professional-looking displays without paying the rates of ad agencies or large studios. Chelsea Design produced this display ad for Mertack's to use in local community newspapers.

have a good income. Some companies are dropping or scaling back on these media. And if you work for ad agencies, you're likely not to get paid until after the agencies have been paid.

Corporate Identity

This field encompasses the logos and other graphic statements that distinguish corporations in the minds of the public. It also includes letterhead, business cards and business forms. A company doesn't have to be a corporation to need a corporate identity. Any business, large or small, can benefit from a defining graphic image.

Logos are the most obvious aspect of corporate identity, but the field touches all of a company's advertising and marketing material, from its TV spots to its stationery and business forms. Ideally, a corporate logo is memorable, meaningful and appropriate for the company. The AT&T logo, created by corporate identity guru Saul Bass, is a perfect example. The tech-

Making Employee Newsletters Work

Biz Graphics was born because owner Pat Brooks was helping small businesses talk to the outside world. Today, the company specializes in helping big businesses talk to the inside world.

Brooks was working in advertising and marketing for a high-tech company in Cincinnati but yearned to try something different. She started doing some sideline consulting for the Small Business Development Center of nearby Northern Kentucky University. There, she helped entrepreneurs set up marketing strategies to launch their businesses. "While I was there," she says, "I realized I had all the resources at my disposal and I thought: Why don't I do this? It was the right time for me to leave, because the middle part of the following year, my company started layoffs."

So Brooks launched her own desktop design and publishing business in 1986, with a wide variety of work and clients. She produced marketing brochures, presentation graphics and corporate identity packages for businesses large and small. Work with medium-size clients on collateral materials led to work on some employee newsletters. That, in turn, led to referrals to larger corporations that needed help with their newsletters. And it soon became clear that her best market was one she never anticipated: employee newsletters for medium-size and Fortune 500 companies.

Though corporations would seem likely to have plenty of staff for such projects, she found they often don't. As a result, many companies, even those with in-house desktop design and publishing capabilities, need someone to handle the design and production responsibilities. Sometimes, they need even more.

"I'm trying to get more and more involved in the editorial end of the newsletters," Brooks says. "I want to go into companies and handle it all for them." After managing design and production of the employee newsletter for one of her biggest clients, Brooks sold them on letting her manage the editorial side of the job, too. "Once they see that I can do the job, it's not such a burden for them," she says. Taking over the editorial side not only increases Biz Graphics' billings, but also its control over the projects. "If I handle it myself, I know I can get the publication out on time," she says. That keeps her clients happy, and her cash flow steady.

Biz Graphics is a one-woman company, with Brooks using freelance copywriters to handle most editorial tasks. Much of the newsletter contents come from product introductions, press releases or other documentation provided by the client to rewrite. Otherwise, clients will come up with a list of story ideas, some of which involve interviewing managers or other employees. For clients who keep the editorial work in-house, Brooks always tries to establish a production schedule up front, then gently remind them along the way to keep work flowing. Still, much ends up getting done at the last minute.

Despite the problems, Brooks sees employee newsletters as a market that offers good income, stability and creativity. It also has led to referrals for larger projects, including an employee handbook and a corporate identity package for two Cincinnati companies. "I'm working at my capacity," she says. "My next step is to decide whether I want to bring an employee on board."

no-globe symbol at once portrays the company's global reach and its grounding in technology.

You don't need a computer to create a corporate identity, but it can make things easier. Drawing and page layout programs simplify revising a logo and experimenting with various applications. Still, design ability rather than computer wizardry is the key to creating great corporate identity packages. Where the computer plays a bigger role is taking the logo and applying it to other elements of corporate identity. A total corporate identity package could include:

- Logo
- Letterhead
- Business cards for sales reps and executives
- Invoices and customer statements
- Credit and other application reports
- Brochures and other leave-behinds

Pros: Corporate identity jobs are high-profile pieces that can lead to work in every aspect of a company's promotion and marketing programs. Since every company needs an identity, it's a big market. Letterhead, although unlikely to be updated often, is a must for every company; it's a segment of corporate identity that could sustain your business almost by itself.
Cons: Large corporations often go to ad agencies, large design studios or established corporate identity specialists for this kind of work, so it's hard for you to crack the market. Also, unless it leads to work in other corporate projects, a corporate identity package could be a one-shot deal.
Untapped opportunities: New or small companies with no logos or primitive ones can be good places to approach. Add to that thousands of companies whose identities are decades old and show it. Even a company that never dreamed of commissioning a logo needs the rest of the corporate identity package. Ideally, you can turn every letterhead or business card job into a complete package. Companies that relocate are good targets for redesigning corporate identity. Since the address must be changed anyway, why not update the design, too? The trick is finding the companies before they move. Check local

Business forms are one of the more overlooked aspects of corporate identity, but they can be a profitable addition to jobs that might have included only letterhead and business cards. This form by Corporate Publishing, Inc. was part of a package that also included price lists and other marketing materials.

business papers for news, new lease signings and building permits. You may also want to develop a relationship with building owners and managers, who may be willing to refer new tenants to you.

Business Forms
This is an unglamorous field, but hardly one to overlook if your interest is making money. Banks, insurance companies, dry cleaners or any other businesses that generate application forms or invoices are potential customers. The minute detail involved in creating business forms lends itself perfectly to the desktop designer and publisher's craft. But business forms also can be an art. Incorporating well-designed business forms into companies' corporate iden-

tity packages helps them turn mundane forms into marketing vehicles. And it helps you turn a ho-hum job into an exciting, high-paying one.

The vast array of generic forms available to businesses is perhaps the biggest source of competition. That's why you need to distinguish the forms you create from the rest of the pack. It means being able to create forms that are graphically more appealing and easier to read and use. You can help a business make its forms serve two purposes: channeling information and winning and keeping customers.

Pros: The size of this market, and the fact that it's a way to generate additional business from existing accounts, are its biggest pluses. Business forms are also time-consuming projects that can generate lots of billable hours. As we know by now, the paperless office is a myth. Computers if anything have made it easier for businesses to generate more paperwork faster.

Cons: Business forms are no fun. No matter how hard you push the envelope, there's only so much creativity you can cram into a business form. There may be some people out there with the stamina to do nothing but create business forms, but for most of us, this is more a way to supplement revenue than sustain it.

Untapped opportunities: One way to get into this field is to ask your current business customers about doing their forms. Every letterhead job or corporate identity package is a potential business form job, too. Printers who specialize in business forms might also need your services. Even if they have someone in-house to handle design and pre-press work, they may need someone else to handle peak work loads. The fact that you can be a marketer for them, steering your business form clients their way for printing, is a plus.

Publications

Jacket/cover design, page design and typography are the main jobs book and magazine publishers require. Publishers often handle this work internally. But as the field gets more competitive, it makes sense that more publishers look for outside vendors to help in both areas.

Jacket/cover design is a higher-profile, more glamorous area, but also one where you have little competitive edge over traditional design studios. You do, however, have a definite edge as far as typesetting. And the computer's ability to combine page design, typesetting and paste-up into one job gives them a huge edge over traditional methods in page and section design. Layout and design are pretty simple for a mass-market, text-only book, though managing the huge type files and page breaks is a tough job. Your best opportunities are in working with magazines and illustrated books, such as textbooks and specialty titles.

Obviously it pays to live in a major publishing center such as New York if you plan to make a living in this area. But the major accounts are likely to go to large, well-established studios, anyway. Most mid-to-large-size cities have at least one or two book publishers or university presses, and there's plenty of work from smaller publishers that can help you build a portfolio to win bigger accounts. Also, modems and faxes have made it much easier for designers outside of New York to service publishing accounts. And with the right contacts and skills, breaking into work for book publishers is quite possible.

Most major cities have a city magazine, a chamber of commerce publication, several trade or professional organization magazines and a smattering of specialty magazines. Often these publications are short-staffed and very much in need of outside vendors for design. Your customers could also be smaller publications that don't want to make the outlays in equipment and training for desktop design and publishing but still want to take advantage of the technology.

Pros: Even for a job that involves little more than straight text, typesetting a book is complicated. Page breaks, fitting copy to meet budgeted page counts, and frequent font changes make this job more than just a matter of wading through monstrously long files. As a result, billings can be better than they might appear at first glance. Design and layout of illustrated books is a high-end, high-profile job. Since even medium-size publishers handle fifty or more titles a year, the potential work volume is good. Work on books also can lead to other types of jobs from publishers, such as catalogs, mailers, bulletins and store displays.

Magazine accounts can mean steady, high-

Not all magazine accounts are huge Manhattan-based publications. Jane Scarano of Data Search Publications handles page layout and design for *Wizard*, a magazine based in Nanuet, New York, aimed at comic book buffs.

profile work, with plenty of room for creativity and professional development. You may start with production aspects and add design functions as the client begins to trust your judgment more.

Cons: There are relatively few book publishers, with the majority concentrated in New York City. Mergers have decreased their numbers significantly in recent years, though economic pressures also have led to more use of outside contractors. On the magazine side, the efficiency of combining editorial and design functions in one system puts pressure on publications to bring electronic design and production in-house. The boom in magazine start-ups in the eighties was followed by a bust in the nineties, with numerous failures and falling profits among even healthy publications. So clients in this field could be dwindling, and many of those hanging on have become slower at paying outside contractors.

Untapped opportunities: Besides typesetting, most nonfiction books need indexes, too. Publishers generally contract with outside indexers. The advent of specialized indexing programs can make indexing and typesetting a natural fit, which means you could offer your services in both as a package deal. Also, self-publishing is a perfect area for desktop designers and publishers. Hundreds of authors self-publish books each year, and need outside vendors to produce almost all of them. Though self-publishers are a diverse group that's hard to target, business consultants are a good place to start. Their books make great leave-behinds to impress prospective clients—but the book needs to look

Veteran Designer Aims at High-End Publishing

Robert Creager was a graphic artist for more than thirty years before he got interested in computers in 1979. He was among the first graphic artists in America to use desktop design and publishing when he experimented with a service called "Personal Publishing" through "The Source," a now-defunct computer network service. Despite his pioneering efforts and the ten years he taught at the Columbus (Ohio) School of Art and Design, Creager isn't interested in teaching people anymore.

Thanks to his years of experience and considerable reputation, the Westerville, Ohio, freelance designer no longer has to. In fact, he has a luxury many designers don't: being selective about his clients. He hasn't done any formal marketing since the seventies, when he owned his own large studio. Even then, he made only one cold call a year. And he eventually closed the studio when he realized that he was a lot better at design than at managing people.

Creager now works almost exclusively for major book and magazine publishers, and entirely on referral. Two major book publishers are clients in part because they invested in proprietary desktop design and publishing systems that are so little known that it's hard to recruit employees to work with them. But otherwise, his clients are savvy, high-end accounts. And even though Westerville is remote from publishing centers, Creager's long-time connections in design and his 9,600-baud modem help bridge the gap.

Creager's services are mostly limited to design, such as jacket and page design and type specing. "I'm basically a designer, though I do some production work," he says. "But when I get into production work for a publisher, it's usually in the marketing end on catalogs, not in the manufacturing end with books. My rates are just plain too high for book manufacturing. Nobody pays designer rates for pasting up or typesetting a book. But the catalogs, it's more design on the fly, where you're almost designing the catalog as you're putting it together. You don't have the production people double-checking and triple-checking and proofing."

professional to be impressive. Any magazine in your area that doesn't use desktop design and publishing is a potential client. Don't overlook small specialty publications and trade journals, who won't likely be courted by major studios.

Newspapers

Inch for column inch, newspapers represent a bigger market than either magazines or books. But for most metropolitan dailies handle almost all typesetting and page design in-house, since the editorial copy is already computerized. Plus, the urgency of meeting daily deadlines doesn't exactly lend itself to working with outside vendors.

Nonetheless, you can find a place in newspaper publishing. Even large, fully electronic daily newspapers may want to farm out work on special sections, Sunday magazines and the like. Unlike the main, run-of-press sections, these sections are planned months in advance and produced sometimes days or weeks in advance. Editorial work is often handled by freelancers or is "canned" copy pulled from a wire service. Since these sections are an extra chore for newspaper staff, they may require costly overtime. So publishers can be persuaded to hand the work over to outside contractors.

Smaller community publications also can be good targets for your work. Usually, these publications don't have the money or the volume of work to justify buying their own graphics computer equipment and hiring their own staff artists. Their alternative is either to produce their publications inefficiently and unattractively — or contract your services. You can make a big difference in these publications' ability to compete for ad dollars with bigger, more fully staffed papers.

Another good market is newspaper information graphics. True, large dailies have in-house designers who can handle these graphics, and wire services increasingly offer sophisticated graphics with their stories. But smaller dailies and weeklies rarely have in-house editorial graphics departments that can handle these duties, and they use fewer wire services. Newspapers of all sizes have been bitten by the *USA Today* bug—that desire to have graphics to help tell virtually every story. Often the graphics are for stories planned days or weeks in advance, so there's time for outside vendors to handle the job. If you can turn around graphics in a day or, occasionally, on a few hours' notice, all the better.

On the high end, newspapers are increasingly interested in digital photo processing. While large dailies are investing in the technology and talent to develop in-house digital darkrooms, smaller dailies and weeklies will look for outside vendors to handle this work.

Pros: Newspapers are a vast market that desktop designers and publishers anywhere can tap. They're a source of constant work once you're established. The jobs permit plenty of creativity and are very high profile, because your graphics carry your credit line. As a rule, newspapers are fast and predictable payers, in good times and bad.

Cons: Newspapers have been hit as hard as magazines by the recession in retail advertising, so budgets are tight in many places. Newspapers in general and smaller-circulation papers in particular aren't the biggest spenders in the world to start out with, so you may not be able to negotiate top dollar for your work. But unlike reporters and editors, desktop designers and publishers aren't pounding down newspapers' doors looking for work.

Untapped opportunities: The entire newspaper industry is an untapped opportunity for the most part—particularly information graphics for smaller dailies and weeklies.

Self-Publishing

Surprisingly, many desktop designers and publishers overlook the niche that would spring to mind immediately from their name: publishing. But some do find success creating and selling their own publication. The options are almost endless. But here are a few categories that are the most promising:

The Desktop Publishers' Publisher

Jane Scarano knew all about the tools of desktop publishing. Not only did she use them for her clients, she sold them to other desktop publishers as a mail-order retailer. What she found lacking was information about business administration and marketing in this increasingly competitive field.

That's why the Valley Cottage, New York, woman started her own newsletter to fill the void. Her newsletter, *Cut & Paste*, is a bimonthly look at business and marketing for desktop publishers, with most of the articles written by owners of their own desktop publishing firms. "There's a great need to understand how to build a desktop publishing business," Scarano says. "There were plenty of publications on techniques and software and design, but nothing on marketing."

Scarano started her newsletter with some informal market research on electronic bulletin boards. "The first step I took was to put up a bulletin on Prodigy (a nationwide commercial computer bulletin board accessed via modem) to throw out the idea for the newsletter to people in desktop publishing clubs," she says. "I asked anybody who was interested to send me their name and address, and I got over 200 responses. I decided there was a definite market for this."

She kept doing on-line market research through desktop publishing forums, posting more bulletins and getting more responses. She created a press release announcing the kickoff of her newsletter, posted it on the bulletin boards and got even more responses. Then she worked out promotional deals with local user groups, desktop publishing magazines, and the National Association of Desktop Publishers, exchanging recommendations with the groups. She also took out an ad in *Home Office Computing* and got her press release published in *Desktop Publisher*. And she bought a mailing list from the latter publication and sent out free sample copies with subscription offers.

Scarano's Data Search Publications has a

toll-free number she answers herself to field inquiries about the newsletter. "As a consumer myself, I knew people were willing to call if it was toll-free," she says. "My experience has been that you get twice the number of inquiries if you have a toll-free number and you offer a free issue." The down side of the toll-free number, she adds, is that it encourages calls from people who have no idea of what they want or no interest in buying. That's been particularly difficult for the retailing side of her operation. In several cases, she's spent up to half an hour on the phone having her brain picked by people whose intention was to buy equipment, software or supplies from someone else. But she still picked up the phone tab. "At the beginning, I went along with it," she says. "Now, I just cut them off."

Scarano uses her Gateway 2000 386 PC Clone, PageMaker 4.0 and HP Laserjet 3 printer to produce mechanicals for her eight-page, two-color newsletter on glossy magazine stock. Thanks to her readership, she has plenty of free advice on ways to improve her presentation. Letters to the editor mostly laud the information or provide ways to tweak the design or push PageMaker to improve the look.

She has a page of advertising in each issue but has mixed feelings about accepting ads. "I want the newsletter to be a substantial kind of thing," she says. "Any product I put in there I want to be something . . . that the public doesn't usually see."

The ads she's sold so far have been from people who approached her rather than the other way around.

The newsletter, launched in 1991, takes up about half of Scarano's time, with equipment and supply sales and her own desktop design and publishing business consuming the rest. For the latter, she designs and produces newsletters for health clubs and professional practices and does typesetting for a magazine on comic books.

Jane Scarano turned to a self-publishing project that was a natural for her—a marketing and business newsletter for desktop publishers.

■ *Community publications*. If your town or neighborhood isn't served by a community newspaper, starting your own is a great way to capture advertising dollars from local retailers who would waste their money trying to reach broader audiences with higher circulations. Even a relatively small neighborhood might be served by a newsletter. If you want to keep time commitment low, a shopper with little or no editorial content is a possibility for a one-person operation.

■ *Specialty publications*. Newspapers or magazines on any area of your expertise are another possibility. Sports publications for a local university, local business newspapers where they don't already exist, or hobby publications are a few examples. Since these publications might come out monthly or less frequently, they're easy to fit into your schedule as a sideline.

■ *Newsletters*. Any subject in which you have special expertise is a possibility. Newsletters are generally high-cost, low-circulation publications geared to a very specialized audience, so quality and timeliness of information is a must.

■ *Special projects*. Some yearbooks and other publications that come out on long cycles can also be money-makers if you can sell advertising based on the lasting impact. One example: a directory of information for new parents about pediatricians, day-care centers, activities, etc. Ads from those same groups are a natural, and distribution can be made through obstetricians' offices, hospitals, childbirth classes or direct mail.

Pros: Becoming a publisher can be either a sideline or a business in itself. There are many opportunities that can develop—for instance, designing ads for advertisers and then moving into other types of jobs for them.
Cons: Publishing just about anything is time-consuming, risky and hard on cash flow. You must make an initial investment in editorial work, production and printing before you bring in any cash for your efforts.
Untapped opportunities: There are thousands. The key is identifying an unfilled need or untapped audience in your community or, in the case of newsletters or other specialty publications, nationwide.

Signage
Desktop designers and publishers are so used to working on smaller printed material that they often miss signs of a great potential market all around them: signage. True, you'll have to work on a scale version in many cases—but that's the same problem traditional designers have. Your advantages in turnaround time and cost can give you the edge in working with retailers and convention/trade show exhibitors—the two key customers in this market.
Pros: This is a huge market, even if you just consider all the retailers who use signs. Products and prices change often, meaning lots of repeat business once you land an account. Trade show exhibits must be changed regularly as well. Doing signage also can lead to other jobs for a client.
Cons: This can be a very cyclical market. Retailers are among the first to feel the pinch when the economy heads south. Overexpansion and heavy debt in the retail industry has wreaked havoc in the nineties, creating a lot of bad credit risks here, though locally based retailers have suffered less. Trade shows, likewise, are one of the first areas companies cut back on during a recession.
Untapped opportunities: The many stores in your area whose signs are ugly or unprofessional are natural targets. Make a couple of examples of what you would do to improve the signage, and show them to the owner.

Catalogs, Menus and More
Catalogs are a great medium for designers and computers. The interplay of text and art involved in producing a catalog is perfect for computer graphics programs. Also, catalogs are much more abundant than you'd imagine. Everyone knows the national catalogs, many of which are so large it makes sense to handle production in-house. But there are also hundreds of smaller consumer catalogs whose yearly page count is low enough that hiring a staff artist doesn't make sense. Yet they must periodically be revised and sometimes completely overhauled. Add to that thousands of business-to-business catalogs used to sell products wholesale, and you have a huge potential market.

Menus are another large category. Like cata-

Convention Signage Spells Success

Gayle Owens started her career with a Miami, Florida, advertising agency and was a designer for various companies before going into business as a freelance designer. That's why the owner of Corporate Publishing Co., Inc. of Loveland, Ohio, sees herself as a generalist. But she's found some promising niches to specialize in along the way.

One of the best ones she discovered after being in business more than four years. A referral from a past client led to a call from Procter & Gamble, the giant Cincinnati-based consumer products company. The company has a world of potential work for desktop designers and publishers, but this time the company wanted something very specific: signs for trade shows. Every trade show is a potential bonanza for her, she says. Large, bannerlike signs are needed to draw people to the booth, smaller signs to inform them about new products, and other signs for prize drawings and demonstrations.

P&G used to work with an ad agency to create and produce trade show signage. "But I can give it to them quicker and cheaper and still do good work," she says. "I don't have all the overhead, all the staff and a whole building of lights to pay for."

Turnaround time can be particularly crucial for trade show signage, she says. Even though dates of shows are known at least a year in advance, a company's product development doesn't always aim at meeting the schedule of a particular show. That means the marketing department may have to put together a presentation on very short notice. "I've had to work through the night a couple of times," Owens says. "But I like to work at night anyway. There's no phone ringing."

Though convention signage may seem fairly cut and dried, it's often anything but. Companies need top-quality signage to compete for the attention of show attendees, many of whom will make important buying decisions for the year. "I can get really creative sometimes," she says. "For instance, some of the shows use chefs for demonstrations of cooking oils and things like that. So I've done big signs with life-size photos of the chefs and information about their credentials or

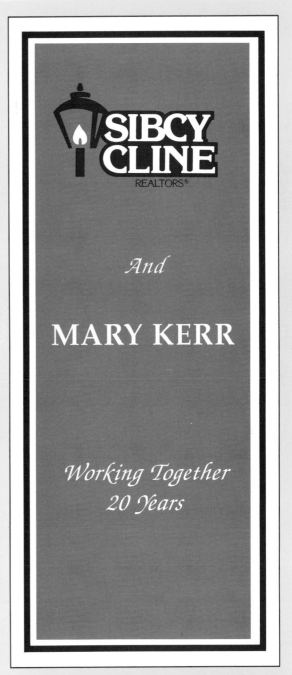

large clocks showing when the next show will be. I make them as bright and eye-catching as I can."

Owens's work has already attracted the attention of a Chicago firm that writes scripts and hires actors and actresses for trade show performances. "They'd been making their own signs

MARY L. KERR
Certified Residential Specialist

PRIVATELY OWNED & OPERATED. . .
Dedicated to the growth and promotion of Greater Cincinnati and Northern Kentucky, resulting in a consistently strong inventory of homes.

MEMBER OF HOMEQUITY...
Which endows Sibcy Cline with a major share of persons transferring into Cincinnati.

FINANCIAL SERVICES...
All office locations with professionally trained staff to assist in qualifying and obtaining prompt loan services.

MARKETING...
Home video service viewed every Sunday at 12 noon on Channel 12, showing a wide range of currently listed homes.

BACKGROUND & ACHIEVEMENTS

☐ Licensed, full-time professional Realtor with Sibcy Cline *20 years*, since 1972.
☐ Million Dollar Club
Cincinnati Board of Realtors, Inc. '78, '80, '81, '83, '84, '85, '86, '87, '88, '89, '90, '91.
☐ Recipient of Certified Residential Specialist designation.
☐ Senior Sales Vice President
☐ President's Sales Club, Ohio Association of Realtors 1988, '89, '90, '91.
☐ Recognized as a corporate leader in Sibcy Cline's TOP CLUB 1986, '87, '88, '89, '90, '91.
☐ Member of Sales and Marketing Council of the Greater Cincinnati Home Builder's Association.
☐ Member of Cincinnati Association of Realtors, Ohio Association of Realtors, and National Association of Realtors.
☐ Well recognized for strong expertise in marketing/negotiating sales of residential properties.
☐ Consistently chosen by large corporations to assist transferring employees.

IN MARKETING YOUR HOME

☐ Confidential meeting with homeowner to discuss and review any necessary repairs or improvement required to best obtain highest market price.
☐ My personal commitment to provide professionally designed brochures and advertisements in your local newspaper, in addition to Sibcy Cline ads in Cincinnati Enquirer.
☐ Submit accurate information promptly to Multiple Listing Service.
☐ Personally conduct "Open House" as mutually determined.
☐ Private tour of your home to familiarize agents prior to showings.
☐ Maintain a strict rapport offering feedback on every showing.

IN SEARCHING FOR A HOME

☐ Provide in-depth information about all areas to assist you in deciding the best location to meet your needs.
☐ Arrange interviews with respective schools.
☐ Provide you with current competitive loan data.
☐ Maintain strong lines of communication with you (and your family) to comfortably adjust to your new home's surroundings.

One overlooked market is real estate agents, who operate as independent contractors and often commission their own marketing materials, such as this brochure by Corporate Publishing, Inc.

with magic markers and things like that," she says. "They do maybe a hundred shows a year and just about all of them need signage. So that looks very promising."

Trade show signs require working on a much larger scale than Owens is used to. Usually she does scale versions with FreeHand and has the final output enlarged by the printer. She sometimes uses service bureaus with color printers for life-size output. But she did one rush job for a manager's meeting of a major hotel chain in which she didn't have the luxury of the enlargement step. She had to design a five-by-four-foot sign in eight pieces in three days. After having the sign printed on foam board, she took the sign to Chicago on a plane. "It took almost as much money to ship it as to make it," she says. "It wasn't fun, but they paid for it."

To help promote her signage and other desktop design and publishing work, Owens has used trade shows herself. She traded some sign work with a promoter of a business show for the printing and graphic arts industries in return for free booth space. As a result, she was able to get hundreds

of dollars' worth of exposure for the $100 she invested in setting up her own booth.

Besides signage, Owens's work involves two other interesting niches: in construction and real estate. For one local builder she designs everything from blueprints and architectural renderings to promotional brochures for finished buildings. She has a background as a marketing and creative director for an engineering department, which helped prepare her for the technical aspect of the work. "They want somebody who can handle it all rather than running from place to place," she says.

Owens also designs one-page brochure/fact sheets for real estate agents' house listings. The sheets serve as memory-joggers for those whose heads spin from seeing dozens of homes. Fast turnaround and the ability to take photos of the homes, too, give Owens—and the agent—an edge. "It amazes me that more Realtors don't use this approach," Owens says. "It's a simple concept, but it can really sell homes."

Paxton Knoll provides, for a select few discriminating buyers, a rare opportunity to reside in one of Hyde Park's most convenient locations.

Situated on a knoll above Paxton Avenue, between Alpine Terrace and Linwood Avenue, Hyde Park Associates has designed a planned development of five individually owned homes. Offered is the privacy of a single-family residence, but the carefree lifestyle afforded by an association-maintained community.

Hyde Park Associates has earned a reputation for developing quality planned communities, with distinctive traditional designs, custom details, and features. Quality and value are the basis of Hyde Park Associates' philosophy.

Corporate Publishing, Inc. created this logo as part of a corporate identity and collateral material package for the Paxton Knoll real estate development in Cincinnati.

logs, they must be changed regularly to adapt to changing prices and selections. Most restaurants cannot afford staff artists, so menus are handled almost always by outside contractors. And since restaurants operate on tight profit margins, they're unlikely to turn to large, high-priced studios or agencies.

Beyond catalogs and menus, almost every manufacturer needs a product list of some kind to distribute to clients. In years past, these may have been fairly plain. But the advent of desktop design and publishing has raised the standard of acceptability. Manufacturers who have no concept of how to meet this demand and no interest in learning how are a great potential market. For many companies, the information to be used on product lists may be part of a computerized database. By subcontracting with a data processing company or specialist, you can increase both your value to customers and your profit.

Pros: This is a huge potential market with lots of repeat business. Setting up the job the first time is usually your client's biggest investment, so he or she has a strong financial incentive to stay with you. Doing something as basic as a product list for a company could build into bigger jobs — such as turning that list into a full-fledged catalog or other marketing materials.

Cons: Depending on the client's needs, this type of work may not leave much room for creativity. It can be little more than a glorified typesetting job, meaning that it's hard to make much money per hour. But the volume and long-term security of the job could make up for that. Smaller clients, such as some restaurants, may have extremely low budgets for such work.

Untapped opportunities: Any business or organization that has a database but can't make it easily presentable is a potential client. Since the category is so broad, it may pay to focus on individual industries. Pick one with which you're familiar. Gift or craft shops are one good source of work. Many supplement their business with mail-order catalogs to their clients over the holidays.

Presentation Graphics

This niche — mostly making slide presentations for sales or corporate meetings — has been

MBS Moore Binding Systems

"Your Complete Binding Source"

PRICE LIST
PLASTIC BINDING SYSTEMS & SUPPLIES

11369 B Williamson Road · Cincinnati, Ohio 45241
(513) 247-3000 · FAX (513) 247-3005
TOLL FREE 1-800-669-0633

② Ibico EPK 21 Electric Binding System

EQUIPMENT

①	Ibico Manual Combo	389.00
②	Ibico EPK 21 Electric Binding System	1,695.00
③	Ibico Electric Power Punch EP28	3,295.00
④	GBC Image Maker 2000	395.00
⑤	GBC Image Maker 3000	1,299.00

COVERS

DESCRIPTION	100	500	1000	2500
Clear Plastic Covers - 10 mil. thickness	44.70	36.95	29.95	27.00
Clear Plastic Covers - 7 mil. thickness	41.30	33.95	26.95	23.50
White Gloss Cover Sets	59.75	52.50	41.25	32.75
Sturdy Grain Cover Sets	44.80	39.95	27.95	24.95
Linen Cover Sets	49.40	38.95	30.95	27.15
Leatherette Cover Sets	102.90	84.95	73.50	69.95
Regency Cover Sets	124.00	105.00	91.25	86.00

COVER CUSTOMIZATION

DESCRIPTION	100	500	1000	2500
OFFSET PRINTING				
Run Charge	.55	.25	.15	.09
Additional Charges				
Close Registration	n/a	.08	.04	.02
Bleeds	n/a	.06	.03	.02
Solid	n/a	.13	.06	.04
SILK SCREENING				
Set Up Charge	$35.00			
Run Charge	.99	.56	.40	.35
EMBOSSING & FOIL STAMPING				
Die Charge (One Time)	$55.00 - $100.00			
Run Charge	.92	.28	.20	.18

Effective January 1, 1992

Product lists, such as this one created by Corporate Publishing, Inc., can be quite simple to produce and a great source of income.

booming in recent years. To be competitive, many companies realize they need to turn to pros to put the "bells and whistles" in their slides. As with typesetting and other production work, desktop designers and publishers are quickly cornering this aspect of the market.

Pros: This is a large and potentially high-profile niche with lots of repeat business, since presentations need to be developed for each new product or proposal. This is a peripheral job that some corporate art departments may sidestep; the work is almost always left to the employees preparing the presentation to do—or have done. That leaves plenty of room for you.

Cons: Competition is increasing. Shops specializing in the field, including one franchise operation, have sprung up in several cities.

Untapped opportunities: Any sales or marketing team that doesn't use slide presentations but could improve its appeal by using them is a good target. Individual sales reps may have the authority to pay for slides from their own ac-

counts, so you may not have to go through the corporate hierarchy.

Consulting

Those who can do, can consult. Corporations setting up in-house computer graphics operations may want your expertise both in choosing equipment and in training employees to use it. Your services, while not cheap, may still be more economical than making big mistakes or using the training centers that specialize in this work. If you do your job well, you can save your clients more in the long run than they will pay you up front. The savings will come from more appropriate equipment selection and fewer hours wasted fumbling around in the new system. You can sell yourself by analyzing and quantifying how much you can save a client.

Developing a niche within a niche is important here. Nationwide companies have a lock on much of the consulting and training business. But they may have little knowledge of the special needs of a particular industry or group. You could, for example, use your expertise to help set up a system for design studios.

Pros: Consulting is easy to fit in as a sideline without taking too much time away from your other business. Fees are high compared to most other jobs, so there's room to undercut the competition and still make good money.

Cons: Because it's easy to add "consulting" to a business card without investing any additional capital or time, the competition in this field keeps getting steeper. Consulting also cannibalizes your business in the long run, since every client you help set up in desktop design and publishing is a client who may not need your services anymore.

Untapped opportunities: This market is well tapped, but one possibility is a computer store that lacks staff with expertise in desktop design and publishing (which isn't hard to find). Offer your services as a consultant, and the store can either refer clients to you or, on a retainer or fee-for-service basis, let you handle customer support calls. You might even serve as a training consultant for the sales staff. Bartering your services in return for new equipment or software is a good way to help the store avoid a cash outlay.

Résumés: Making Them Work for You

Resumes are an enormous market that many desktop designers and publishers tap. But it's not the most promising niche for many reasons. First, print and copy shops can handle this work relatively cheaply. Second, résumés are low-profile work that in many cases won't lead to much advancement. Nonetheless, they're a good entry-level niche. You must offer top-notch design to distinguish yourself from the corner copy shop.

The size and easy entry of this market are the main drawing points. There's some potential for repeat business from keeping résumés on file and updating them. Résumé jobs could occasionally lead to bigger and better things when your clients find jobs. More often, though, it will be a customer service you'll do to keep existing clients happy.

On the other hand, résumés are small-ticket jobs for which administrative and sales tasks—plus unbillable grief and aggravation—can eat away much of your profits. Since most job-seekers are already out of work, they're not great credit risks. It's wise to get your money up front.

Positioning yourself in the high end of the market as an executive résumé service may help eke out a higher income. Networking with employment agencies could be a low-cost way of generating business.

Chapter Three

How to Find Clients

Marketing is a job most people hate. Fortunately, after the initial months or years of business, desktop design and publishing operations often have as much business as they can handle. What marketing they need seems to come from their customers in the form of praise and referrals.

So why worry about marketing? Here are several reasons:

1. Beginners usually don't have the luxury of hanging up a shingle and waiting for business to roll in. Though many can rely on contacts from past jobs, others have to struggle.

2. Even established operations may quickly need to put a marketing plan into action when they lose key accounts. That's especially true if you depend on one major client for most business. No matter how secure you may be with that client, it pays to have a plan in your back pocket.

3. You may have all the business you can handle but still want to branch into new areas. A more diverse client base can protect you from the economic risks of being tied too closely to one industry. A client or two outside your main area of expertise gives you a more versatile portfolio.

4. You may want to improve the quality of your work by improving the quality of your clients. You may be supporting yourself with clients who provide low-end, low-paying but high-volume work; better-quality jobs could get you off that treadmill. Marketing efforts might increase the quality and profitability of your work.

The Perils and Pleasures of Having One Big Client

The logical client base for small desktop designers and publishers would seem to be other small businesses, or lots of big businesses with small jobs. But some desktop designers and publishers report success from basing their business on one big client. The advantage is that it takes a lot less time to prepare one $30,000 invoice than to prepare thirty $1,000 invoices. Steady work from a big corporation eliminates the need to constantly drum up one-time jobs from small accounts. Plus, big accounts are impressive to other prospective clients.

But the perils can be as big as the client. When a client who makes up more than half your business hiccups, you feel an earthquake. Even small downturns or cost-cutting measures can have a major effect on your income. A glitch in the accounting department that delays your check for a few weeks can have disastrous effects on your cash flow. And losing the account can put you under altogether. At worst, basing your business on one big client is like being an employee, only without the benefits or the security afforded by labor laws and unemployment compensation.

None of this prevents Icon Graphics of Roches-ter, New York, from treasuring its major client, Eastman Kodak. Icon, a two-person firm made up of partners Steve BonDurant and Keith Meehan, handles package design and some point-of-purchase materials for the consumer products giant. Slowdowns at Eastman Kodak have a big effect on the business, BonDurant says, but Icon still has enough other business and low enough overhead to ride out storms. To diversify its business beyond Eastman Kodak and beyond Rochester, Icon has advertised in the *Creative Black Book*, a national directory of creative services providers.

Relying on a big client is "scary and reassuring at the same time," says Brian Bauer, whose one-man Digital Design gets most of its business from North Country Corp., a catalog mail-order company. "It's nice having 80 percent of my income that I don't have to scramble for," he says. "And they like my work. However, if they had any major problems, I would be hard pressed to replace them quickly."

Most of Bauer's other jobs are small ones that come through referrals by family and friends in Boston or Cape Cod. They range from letterhead and business cards for a carpenter to a brochure for a conservation group.

5. It may be time to expand. There's a limit to how much a one- or two-person operation can grow, even with freelance help. To support employees, you must keep plenty of work coming in the door.

Finding Potential Clients

Finding a client means thinking like a client. Ask yourself why someone might need your services. Specifically, think why a company or organization would vend out desktop design and publishing rather than handle it in-house. That will help you identify the most likely markets for your talent and steer you away from the blind alleys of marketing.

Level of Need

Consider whether a company or organization has a constant need for design and production services. Does it have enough work to hire a staff artist? If not, the company could be right for your services. A firm that produces one or two brochures and a quarterly employee newsletter each year doesn't need a staff artist. Nor would it need high-priced help from an ad agency or large design studio. Your services would be perfect.

It's difficult to identify companies with low-volume design needs. Driving by the office or looking in the Yellow Pages won't tell you much. One good if time-consuming way to find out is to focus on ten or so local companies and research them in your library, in trade magazines or by networking. Here are a few general clues to finding companies that could be right:

- Small- to medium-size companies are your best bet. Larger companies are more likely to hire a graphic artist.
- Promotion-intensive industries, like consumer products companies, are more likely to have in-house artists.
- Companies with one or two main products are more likely to have only occasional needs than a company with many products.
- Small service concerns are good candidates—from maid services to professionals such as dentists.

Keep in mind that even companies with staff artists can be good customers. But the work they provide and the people you approach will be different. Instead of working directly with the marketing manager on a brochure, you may work with the art department to help with a peak work load.

Seasonal, Occasional Needs

Companies likely to have seasonal or occasional needs for design and production also are good marketing targets. For some small- and medium-size companies, promotions are geared toward one or two trade shows or special events each year.

Some other seasonal or occasional needs to watch for include:

- *Christmas.* The holiday season brings peak promotional demands not only for major department store chains but also for a variety of other retailers and businesses—who will send out specialized Christmas greetings to clients and employees.
- *Tourist season.* If you live in a resort area, hotels, restaurants and tourist attractions may need to redo promotional materials for the new season.
- *Tax season.* Accountants and financial planners are among the professionals who have heavy marketing needs in the months leading up to April 15.
- *Anniversaries.* Companies may want to celebrate a twenty-fifth, fiftieth or one hundredth anniversary with a special publication for employees or promotion for clients.
- *Mergers and acquisitions.* Takeovers and mergers create a huge demand for new marketing materials to explain the changes that result from the restructuring.
- *Change in management.* Key management changes may signal the company is about to clean house in terms of promotional materials and design services, too. The effect may not be immediate. But within about a year, new management will want to change the look and perhaps improve the cost effectiveness of the company's promotional efforts.
- *New businesses.* A new business needs one of everything. Most entrepreneurs will already

have ordered letterhead, business cards and other trappings of company identity before setting up shop. But they also may run into unexpected needs after opening, or discover that their first batch of material doesn't work the way they'd hoped.

Special or Annual Events

Special events held once or even a few times a year are perfect examples of occasional needs for which clients turn to desktop designers and publishers. Such events need to be promoted, but they don't require a year-round staff person. You can position yourself to get this business well in advance of the event.

One way is simply to contact companies or organizations about upcoming events, promotions, fundraisers, etc. Your local chamber of commerce or visitor's bureau may also have a list of some of the larger events held each year. Also, keep a log of events in your area as they happen. That way you can anticipate them next year. Keep this database on your computer and update it as needed. Your newspaper's calendar of events presents a wealth of information. And you can also find events just by keeping your eyes open around town.

Get copies of what promoters are using this year, and be prepared to suggest improvements and submit a bid several months in advance of the next event. Not only does such work provide a nice infusion of income each year, it also can get your work noticed by thousands of people who attend the events.

Here are some of the special events that could generate business:

■ *Festivals and fairs*. Churches, schools and other organizations hold fairs each year, and most are promoted through posters, fliers and ads. Craft shows are another possibility. Special festivals put on by cities and towns may also be good clients.
■ *Fundraisers*. Most charitable organizations have a major fundraising event each year that may need promotional materials.
■ *Sales and special promotions*. Many businesses plan sales on a fairly predictable schedule for holidays or preinventory clearance.

Restructuring and Layoffs

As anyone who's been "restructured" out of a job knows, this is usually a code word for layoffs and early retirement. True, there's some actual restructuring going on, but almost always with an eye toward cutting head counts in the employee cafeteria.

As hard as it is on employees, corporate restructuring does create opportunities for you. Staff reductions in the graphic arts, marketing and personnel departments all leave less time for handling desktop design and publishing tasks, even if the company owns the equipment. Austerity measures may involve cutting back use of outside vendors at first, but when business eventually picks up, there are fewer employees around to pick up the slack. And since many of the staff reductions of the nineties are meant to be permanent, companies will have no choice but to increasingly use outside vendors.

Approaching a company immediately after staff reductions isn't good timing. Besides looking ghoulish, it's less likely to work. The reductions may have been made on the theory that they wouldn't create a need for outside vendors, and contract work often goes to former employees. A year or so after staff reductions may be a better time to approach a company. By then, management has had more time to assess needs. Former employees have more likely moved on to other things. And it may be easier for you to tell if the restructuring was a brilliant strategic move or a blunder that's hastening the company's decline.

New Laws and Regulations

New laws and regulations often create demand for a host of changes in forms, signage, packaging and more. Meeting the sudden needs generated by new rules is often too big a job for the affected companies and the designers and printers they regularly use.

One example is the Nutrition Labeling and Education Act and related regulations, which could force food processors to change labels for about 40,000 products by 1993. Advertising and collateral materials could also be affected. It would make sense to redesign packaging at the same time the nutrition information is changed, but that task will overwhelm staff artists and outside contractors. Both the companies and their vendors will need outside help, including freelancers like you.

Another example is the Americans with Disabilities Act. This sweeping law, passed in 1989 and effective in 1992, was designed to fully open employment and public accommodations to the disabled. In doing so, it forces rewriting of virtually every employee handbook in the United States. It also sets new rules for making signs in public places more readable for people with impaired vision. That will force reworking of signage for many businesses, including hotels, restaurants and stores.

By keeping tabs on such laws and regulations, you can anticipate major changes that could create needs for your services. You can position yourself to get business by contacting affected companies before the regulations take effect.

Narrowing Your Focus: Finding Clients in Specific Industries

Your skills probably are flexible enough to help people in a wide range of fields. But there are some advantages to focusing your efforts on particular industries. One is simple manageability. Unless you live in a very small town, targeting every type of business is virtually impossible. You'll set yourself a marketing task that's so big you may never muster the energy to tackle it. By focusing on a single industry or a few industries, you channel your efforts and money more effectively. This way, you've chosen a handful of trade organizations to join, trade publications to subscribe to, companies to mail to, issues to track, etc.

A second advantage is credibility. You can probably work for a tire manufacturer as well as a real estate developer, but you'll be more convincing to companies in either category if you have a track record in their industry. Every trade has its own jargon, concerns and quirks. By learning those, you'll be better at understanding your clients' needs and how to hit their customers' hot buttons. You don't need to specialize in one very narrowly defined industry. But having significant work from a range of closely related industries, such as several manu-facturers or financial professionals, can help show similar clients how you can help them.

The disadvantage to specializing is that you tie your fate directly to that of the industry. If it hits the skids, so may your business. The solution isn't necessarily to become a generalist but to branch into a handful of industries. Here are some tips for spotting potential clients in a variety of industries or segments.

Ad Agencies

Smaller agencies are more likely to need freelance desktop design and publishing help, or to vend out all such needs. For some reason, an amazing number of medium- to large-size agencies have been slow to jump on the desktop computer bandwagon in many cities. And hard times for the industry in recent years just increase pressure to keep overhead low. Before you get in too deep with an agency, find out who its major clients are and assess their economic health. Also, contact some other independent contractors for the agency, such as copywriters or photographers, to discreetly inquire about payment practices. You may find some agencies are much more eager to give you work than to give you money for it.

Public Relations/Marketing Communications

As a rule, public relations or marketing communications businesses are smaller than ad agencies and more likely to use freelance desktop designers and publishers. Marketing communications companies, which combine market research, ad agency, design and public relations functions, have become popular in recent years. Because they combine several functions, they're a little less susceptible to economic swings than less-diversified firms. And that could make them more stable clients, too. To an extent, public relations and marketing communications companies are a hedge against bad economic times, because it costs less to promote through them than through ad agencies.

The Corporate World

A company's size is one indicator—though not always a reliable one—of how good a potential client it may be. You may assume that a large corporation has a big art department that can

CARDIOVASCULAR CARE CENTER

David B. Southren, M.D., F.A.C.C.
87 Route 303
Valley Cottage, NY 10989
(914) 268-0880

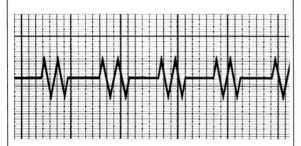

Welcome

We are pleased that you have chosen to let us help you care for your heart. Please take a few minutes to read this brochure. It tells you all about Cardiovascular Care Center, our special services and how we can help you.

Cardiovascular Care Center

Our procedures range from Doppler and Echo Cardiography Testing (non-invasive, or external views, of valvular and muscle anatomy and function) to heart monitoring and heart rhythm analysis to the sophisticated technology of cardiovascular/cardiopulmonary and exercise cardiography procedures.

Cardiovascular/Cardiopulmonary Exercise Testing

This test helps detect coronary artery disease and many other abnormalities of the heart as well as assess an individual's cardiovascular, pulmonary, metabolic and muscular capacity for exercise. It aids in determining an exercise program most suited for your heart's needs. Patients with heart disease or suspected disorders can benefit from its quantitative analysis as it provides unique information about functional significance.

Exercise Echocardiography

The echocardiogram during exercise enables the heart muscle to be viewed and deterioration in muscle function due to inadequate oxygen supply readily detected, independent of the EKG or even symptoms. In addition, the degree of impairment of the muscle can be measured. This provides a useful degree of information previously obtained with more invasive nuclear studies such as the stress thalium studies, which are more expensive and require the injection of radioactive dye during the study as well as a few hours of imaging after the exercise test is over. This test is performed on a bicycle or treadmill and echocardiographic images are obtained before, during and shortly after the test. Often, a preliminary assessment of the results is available during this visit.

We Care For Your Heart

It is of the utmost importance that individuals be aware of the risk factors for cardiovascular disease, such as smoking, hypertension, or elevated cholesterol. Exercise is the best way to control cardiovascular risk factors, reduce stress, improve self image and provide more energy.

Our facility is dedicated to provide state-of-the-art cardiovascular assessment and diagnostic services as well as guide the individual to incorporate cardiovascular healthy life-style and health activities to meet the needs of the rapidly changing concepts of health and disease. We feel that disease treatment must go hand in hand with health direction. To this end we are committed to active patient education and support that includes our newsletter and patient educational materials.

We are dedicated to arresting heart disease and improving cardiovascular health in the context of whole body well being. We provide state-of-the-art testing and take special interest in exercise physiology. Please feel free to discuss any procedure with us and let us help you with any concerns you may have.

Office Hours

Our staff schedules our office hours by appointment only. Our office is always on call and you can reach us at (914) 268-0880.

Emergencies are responded to immediately and you are encouraged to call us days, nights, and weekends. We are available 7 days a week, 24 hours a day. Non-emergency calls are returned as quickly as possible. However, since our busiest time is during the daytime hours, the majority of non-emergency calls are returned after hours. When calling to set up an appointment, please state whether you are calling for an emergency or non-emergency situation.

Hospitalization

More extensive evaluation and therapy requiring hospitalization, such as cardiac catheterization, angioplasty and coronary bypass procedures are closely and actively treated by Dr. Southren as well as by associated specialty teams of doctors, surgeons and staff.

Payment

Payment is requested at time of service. In some instances, other arrangements can be made. If for some reason you can't pay your bill on time, please tell our receptionist, and we'll do our best to work out a payment plan with you. Payments that are delinquent and are unduly late will be turned over to our attorney for processing and collection.

Insurance

Please remember that private health insurance policies are considered a method of reimbursing the patient for fees paid to the doctor and is not a substitute for payment. Any financial benefits that you may receive from insurance are a matter of settlement between you and the insurance carrier. We offer advice and assistance in submitting insurance plans and provide a computer-generated system to help you receive maximum benefits and ease in requesting them.

Vol. 1, No. 1

Women's Health HIGHLIGHTS

Compliments of Dr. Nancy T. Banks, M.D., F.A.C.O.G.

SPECIAL FEATURE

Sexually Transmitted Diseases

Magic Johnson tests HIV!!!! Shock; Dismay. Those were the first reactions. The denial mechanism is now setting in... "But you know these athletes, they are so promiscuous. Fact: Your sexual contacts include all of your partner(s) sexual contacts.

NEWS briefs

We are very pleased to announce that on January 29th, Michelle Mosner, R.D., who has a B.S. in Nutritional Sciences from Cornell University, joined our staff as a nutrition consultant.

Our goal is to help you maintain optimum health for a long and productive life. To that end, Michelle will be available to address your nutritional and dietary needs. You can make an appointment with her through our office by calling (914) 353-3100.

The diet of North Americans has changed significantly since 1900. Then, most meals were based upon grain products, potatoes, fresh vegetables and fruits — with meats consumed only occasionally. In recent years we have replaced this dietary style, rich in complex carbohydrates and fiber and low in fats and cholesterol, with a high-fat, low-fiber diet largely based upon meats, dairy and other animal products.

By 1980, consumption of grains and potatoes fell to half their 1900 levels, while the amount of fats in the American diet more than doubled. Such drastic dietary changes cannot occur without very significant consequences — not only in the public health, but in the economy and the environment as well.

Excerpted from the Pulitzer Prize nominated Diet for New America by John Robbins.

What is a sexually transmitted disease? (STD)

Except for the flu and colds, STD's are the most widespread contagious diseases in the United States. They are passed from person to person through SEX. Any close contact that involves the genitals, the mouth or the rectum can transmit STD'S. Some can be cured, some cannot.

These diseases are never harmless. Some can cause serious, even life-threatening problems such as infertility, cancer and AIDS. Many can cause problems during pregnancy or infect a fetus or newborn baby.

Types of Sexually Transmitted Diseases

	Cases per Year in the U.S.
Chlamydia	Four Million Cases
Genital warts	One Million Cases
Gonorrhea	Four Million Cases
Genital Herpes	500,000 Cases
Pelvic Inflammation Disease	One Million Cases
Hepatitis B	300,000 Cases
Syphilis	130,000 Cases
AIDS	199,406 Total U.S. Cases

Preventing Sexually transmitted diseases.
Chlamydia

Chlamydia trachomatous is a bacteria which has long been known as the cause of trachoma, an eye disease common in developing countries. Approximately 500 million people have trachoma. Blindness occurs in 2 million. Genital infections caused by chlamydia (From Greek Word "Chlamys, to Cloak) can result in severe medical problems which can be quite severe in women. It most often starts as a cervical infection which can spread through the uterus and fallopian tubes. This tubal inflammation or salpingitis may block the tubes with scar tissue resulting in infertility or an increased risk of ectopic or tubal pregnancy, a condition that causes 10% of maternal deaths.

continued from page 2

Here are two examples of the types of marketing materials doctors and other health-care providers use. One is a brochure aimed at introducing new patients to the Cardiovascular Care Center in Valley Cottage, New York. The other, for a West Nyack, New York, physician, takes a more indirect approach as a newsletter for patients on current women's health issues.

handle all its needs, or else deals with big-name agencies exclusively. But you'd be surprised how many small desktop designers and publishers work for big companies. Company size may be a better indicator of the types of work you can get than of whether you can get work at all.

Smaller companies, from Mom-and-Pop operations to companies up to one hundred employees, are most likely to look to outside design services rather than have a staff artist; they can provide you with a wide range of business. They're less likely to pay top dollar for major design studios and ad agencies and more likely to look for independent desktop designers and publishers. But they may also assign desktop design and publishing work to secretaries or someone else in the company with little prior design experience.

For larger companies, design functions are more likely to be handled in-house or by an agency. But that doesn't mean you couldn't be a vendor handling peak work loads. Nor does it close you out of all areas of a corporation. The art department may only handle packaging and ad design, leaving collateral material to outside vendors. Even if it handles collateral material, the department's turnaround time may not be fast enough. So sales reps may seek you out for work that needs to be done on short notice. Regional sales offices of large corporations can be particularly good targets, because the supply lines from headquarters may be so long that they're of little help. Likewise, internal communications may have limited access to the art department. Here, too, there's a niche for you. Keep in mind that even big companies don't like to throw money away. They're increasingly turning to desktop designers and publishers to handle tasks that don't require the pricier services of agencies or employees.

One way to approach businesses in general is by taking advantage of promotional conventions. Start with the potential client and work backward to the potential marketing opportunity. First, identify companies you'd like to work for. Then research their industries to identify the key shows and conventions they attend, or any other seasonal factor that influences their promotions. Use trade publications, which should be available at a larger public or university library. Then try a mailing followed by a phone call to the marketing or sales department.

Professionals
Professionals are a large and relatively untapped market. Most professional firms are too small to afford a graphic artist on staff. But they do have needs for design services, ranging from letterhead, business cards and other areas of corporate identity, to direct-mail pieces.

Here's a thumbnail description of the types of clients and work to look for in the following areas:

■ *Health care.* Attitudes about marketing in health care professions range from unbridled enthusiasm to outright disdain. For more promotion-oriented groups, you can expect work in preparing direct-mail packages or display ads. But virtually any medical practice now uses some kind of brochures, if only to inform patients about policies or medical procedures. Chiropractors—followed closely by cosmetic surgeons—are the most eager promoters. Dentists, facing a tougher market than in decades past largely because of their successes, are looking for ways to attract new patients or inform current ones about new procedures and advances. Relatively new specialties—such as sports medicine—may need marketing materials to explain themselves to a public that hasn't heard about them before. Surgeons, however, generally keep a low profile on the marketing front. Whichever office you target, approach a secretary or office manager rather than one of the doctors.

■ *Lawyers.* Restrictions on advertising for this profession are gone. But it's still an ethics violation to solicit individual clients directly. Except for personal injury practitioners, the only marketing vehicles most lawyers are likely to use are reputation and client newsletters. Don't overlook the possibility of handling other work, though, such as corporate identity, documents, and other presentation graphics used as exhibits in trials. Trial exhibits are sometimes very involved and well-designed information graphics describing accident scenes or detailing other events. Larger national or regional firms are more likely to have someone in-house to handle such needs, but private practitioners or small- and medium-size firms may be good potential clients. Managing partners or practice administrators are the people to approach first.

■ *Accountants.* This is another good newsletter market. Not only do accountants need to project a professional image and keep their names in front of clients, but they also have something important to say to them. Reminder notices for customers at tax time are one thing every C.P.A. needs. You may also help them develop their own tax forms on disk, along with custom worksheets to help clients prepare tax and other information. A good newsletter from an accountant can help clients save money year-round and generate business outside of tax season. This is such a dry subject that it needs all the design help it can get. Smaller firms and individual accountants in private practice are the best markets to approach, as larger national firms are more likely to handle marketing centrally.

■ *Business and management consultants.* Many operate solely on word of mouth. But if they use any marketing technique, it's likely to be newsletters. They also need brochures and other leave-behinds for prospective clients. Though numerous, consultants are often harder to find than other professionals. The "Management Consultants" listing in the Business-to-Business Yellow Pages is a place to start. But that doesn't include some consultants who advertise under headings related to their area of expertise, such as systems consultants, security consultants, etc.

■ *Financial planners.* This group includes insurance agents and specialized financial consultants. Like business consultants, they have a strong need to project a professional image. In fact, theirs may be even stronger: Surveys show the quality of the presentation has a major impact on consumers' investment decisions. Though much of their material is prepared by the companies they may represent, financial planners may need to put together specialized packets for key customers. Financial planners also use newsletters heavily to project an authoritative image and keep investment ideas in front of clients.

Nonprofit organizations use as wide a variety of marketing materials as for-profit companies. This brochure for the Westchester Division of the American Cancer Society is directed at potential volunteers.

Nonprofit

Nonprofit groups can be a great potential market. Since most rely on donations or memberships for their livelihoods, the effectiveness of their promotional material is paramount. The need for fundraising letters and communications with members creates a constant need for graphic arts services. For many groups, the need is substantial enough for a full-time graphic artist. But others vend out work. The catch is the group may not be able or willing to pay much. Your pay, however, can go well beyond monetary compensation and the sense of doing good. Working for nonprofit clients also can provide great exposure and experience for new and seasoned designers alike. Nonprofit clients also afford you creative freedom seldom available elsewhere, which can more than offset low or no pay.

The nonprofit heading includes a variety of organizations. They include:

■ *Charitable organizations.* These include the community chest, local food banks or national charities that may be based in your area. Marketing your services to truly needy organizations can be a losing battle economically, since even if you get a client, you may not want to charge your normal rate. For better-off organizations, however, it might make sense. If it fits your skills, database management for contributors and members is a related service you could provide.

■ *Places of worship.* You may want to donate your efforts to your own congregation but have no qualms about charging others a fair price. Therefore, marketing to churches and synagogues you're not affiliated with may be a better idea. Bulletins and newsletters, often the duty of the clergy or secretary, are the work a larger congregation will most likely need.

■ *Trade and professional organizations.* Supported by dues-paying companies and professional members, these groups publish a variety of materials aimed at keeping membership rosters full and members informed of industry trends. National headquarters handle much of the work. Most headquarters have full-time staff to handle communications, but they may need help at peak times, such as conventions.

Even local chapters may have newsletters that require outside desktop design and publishing help (often it's easier to raise cash than to get donations of time from members). Look under "Organizations" in your Yellow Pages, plus the *Gale Encyclopedia of Associations.*

■ *Arts organizations.* Most demand the highest quality presentations because their members and contributors are artistically astute. Yet these groups are usually underfunded and have neither the staff, equipment nor money to buy high-priced design for promotional materials. Your ability to provide a high-end look for a low-end price can be a major selling point. Donating your work to such groups may pay off

St. Stephen's Episcopal Church

**9191 Daly Road
Cincinnati, Ohio 45231
(513) 522-8628**

*St. Stephen's Episcopal Church
Cincinnati, Ohio*

Welcome to St. Stephen's Episcopal Church. We are a neighborhood church, drawing people from all over the county. We are not saints, nor perfect; we are simply friendly people searching together for God. Through our faith in Jesus Christ we care for, share with, and support each other day by day.

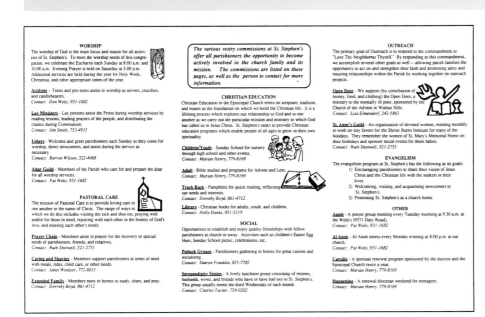

Places of worship are an often overlooked source of business for desktop publishers. Their needs range from weekly bulletins to display ads to brochures for new members or visitors.

not only in terms of philanthropy, but by exposing your work to a very upscale audience.

■ *Local politicians and political groups*. National and statewide efforts usually retain specialty agencies to handle their campaigns. But local candidates are easier to target. Involvement in local politics is the best way—and often the only way—to enter this market. Even on the local level, campaigns have a wide range of funding and sophistication. Some are managed by professional campaign managers and use extensive direct mail; others are on shoestring budgets. But even the smallest suburban races may require brochures and mailers.

Government Agencies

Any sector that takes up more than a quarter of the Gross National Product is not to be overlooked. And the trend toward privatization of government services in the eighties has made the opportunities better. But finding them still can be difficult. Here are some places to look:

■ *Schools*. Local school districts can be a good source of business, and one often overlooked by desktop designers and publishers. Virtually every school district publishes an annual report. Many districts and some individual schools also publish newsletters for parents. Smaller city and suburban districts are more likely to turn to outside vendors, while larger urban districts are more likely to have a communications staffer. (Note: Because private schools must market themselves to parents, they are often an even better potential market than public schools.)

■ *Local government*. Your municipal, county or town government may be the best bet in the government sector, because it's much easier to work your way through the bureaucracy maze. Communications or public affairs offices are one place to check. You also can try the city or county administrator or manager. As with political campaigns, connections working in local politics would be a major plus. Agencies with lots of direct public contact—such as public welfare, children's services, public and mental health, senior services, civil defense, parks and recreation—are the most likely to issue brochures and publications that require your help. Quasi-public institutions are often particularly promotion-minded. These include some human service agencies, such as senior and youth services, that are actually private, nonprofit entities under contract to local governments. Promotion for them is a matter of survival, because renewal of their contracts can depend on public support.

■ *Colleges and universities*. Higher education generates huge amounts of promotional material. Often it's by students, faculty or someone in-house, but many institutions use outside contractors for much of the work. Offices or departments of external relations, admissions, athletics, public relations, public information or community outreach are among those that use outside design help—often independently of one another. Even individual academic departments may handle their own promotional efforts for special events—particularly creative and performing arts departments.

■ *State government.* Based on size alone, your state government is a little more approachable than federal government. Living in the state capital is an obvious plus. But agencies located in outlying cities may also need your services. Some states offer information on procuring state contracts through a development, commerce or small business department. Unfortunately, while they may be privatizing more, states aren't going out of their ways to find smaller vendors. Former state employees and companies with political or personal connections to agencies have the inside track.

■ *Federal government.* You won't get too far here by knocking on doors. The vast array of agencies and the immense bureaucracies make finding potential federal customers difficult. And the fact that most government publication design work is handled in-house would make your efforts even more fruitless. Probably the best tactic is to review *Commerce Business Daily*, a newspaper published by the U.S. Department of Commerce and available in most

Having a Specialty and Using Contacts Pays Off

Gail Silverman went into business for herself out of self-defense rather than design. In 1984, she found herself out of a job when the *Journal of Cardiovascular Medicine,* a monthly magazine for which she was art director, folded. She started freelancing until she could find a staff position, but she liked freelancing so much, she decided to stick with it.

Silverman has built her New York City-based business with little formal marketing. But her clients have included big names such as The New York Times Co. and McGraw-Hill Publishing Co. She started by tapping the resources closest at hand—friends and business associates. "Early on, I would pump people for names of anyone they knew, just to get in the door," she says. "I made some cold calls, and I always found that if I had a name, I did much better in terms of initial reception." Once she got in the door, her portfolio was strong enough to win most jobs she needed, though one client paid her to do a trial brochure before hiring her for additional work.

Sticking with her niche in health care has brought her most of her business, she says. "I try to stick with the medical area because I feel that's where I have the best chance of getting work," Silverman says. "That's what I have to show and

what I get the most response from."

Her major client is Marion Merrell Dow, a pharmaceutical company she was referred to by an associate at her former employer. Word of mouth or contacts based on tips from friends have led to jobs with another pharmaceutical firm, two bimonthly medical publications and two hospitals.

After several years of freelancing, Silverman has as much business as she can handle as a one-woman studio operating from her home. Now, her efforts center around maintaining good relations with clients and letting them know about new services she can offer. For example, when she first used Adobe Photoshop and output to film, Silverman called her longstanding clients to tell them how the new procedure would help her accommodate their rush orders. "Clients are always interested in hearing what new things I'm doing," she says.

"Things haven't gotten slow enough the last couple of years that I had to approach anybody," she says. But in case business ever does take a downturn, Silverman has a sketch of a promotional piece on file that she could turn out fairly quickly. "It basically shows magazine covers and interior covers that I was going to use to sell my work in the medical community. It's always in the back of my mind that I can update it and print it if things get slow."

main libraries. It's a comprehensive listing of all products and services offered or wanted by U.S. government agencies, along with specifications on whom to contact or how to bid.

Hospitals/Health Care

Since they don't compete on price, hospitals compete through technology, service and promotion. Volume of the latter is so heavy that even midsize cities sometimes have agencies that specialize in health care accounts. Work includes magazines, brochures, newsletters, direct mail and more. Obviously, there's a big enough market here for all types of vendors to compete, including you. Hospital communications, marketing or public relations departments are the key contacts. The health-care industry is diverse and growing: Don't overlook urgent-care facilities, nursing homes, home nursing services and related agencies.

Restaurants

Menus and direct mail for restaurants combine to form a fairly substantial market. Unfortunately, few individual clients or jobs generate enough income to warrant a full-fledged marketing effort. The best way to tap this market is to position yourself to get as many restaurant customers as possible with as little outlay of time and expense. Casually let owners of restaurants you frequent know who you are and what you do. Teaming up with a restaurant supplier might also be a good idea. Food service or restaurant equipment wholesalers—who always look for ways to broaden their services to customers—might be interested in brokering your services to their clients.

Retailers

Local and single-unit retailers are your best bet, since larger chains are more likely to have in-house staff or agencies. Boutiques and specialty shops can be very good customers. They're likely to keep mailing lists of their customers and keep in touch through newsletters and periodic special offers. Some may even publish their own catalogs. And because they have a high-end image to maintain, they're less likely to risk cranking out amateurish-looking pieces on their own. Telling the owners of stores you shop at what you do is a relatively painless way to tap this market. You can also target mailings to these shops fairly easily by checking Yellow Pages listings.

Commercial Printers

Printers aren't just important for getting out the end product. They're also important customers and marketers for your work. Some desktop designers and publishers have developed the majority of their business through referrals from printers. Your relationship with your printer can be wonderfully symbiotic: They provide clients or overflow work, you broker business to them or send customers to them directly.

You may see printers as competition, especially the plethora of quick-print shops. An increasing number offer desktop design and publishing services as a way to maximize their sales. But you can make printers your friends. One logical step is finding printers in your area who don't already have desktop design and publishing services, and forming an alliance. They may want to refer customers to you directly or pay you as a vendor. Either way, it's probably going to be more economical for them than increasing overhead by adding an employee to do desktop design and publishing. Even printers who already offer these services can be your partners. Like any business, they have times when they're

---

The baby has arrived . . .

The family is settled in . . .

And now it's time to get back to work!

Announcing the return of . . .

VICKI WILLIAMS

to . . .

ALL ABOUT HAIR
1517 Springfield Pike
Wyoming

Beginning June 26, 1991.
Call 761-5313 now for an appointment.

Small retail operations require a number of marketing and collateral materials, such as this announcement for a hairstylist at All About Hair in Wyoming, Ohio.

Selling to Salespeople

One of the quickest ways into some major corporations is through the sales department door. Sales reps often have limited access to the corporate art department for two reasons: They're in the field and away from headquarters, or their needs rank lower on the totem pole than those of the marketing and advertising departments. Yet sales reps usually have authority to pay you directly through their expense accounts, which can be great for cash flow.

Among the needs sales reps frequently have are:

- Typesetting for specialized proposals
- Collateral materials for new products
- Fliers or brochures for booths at trade shows
- Slides and other presentation graphics

Successful tactics for tapping business from sales reps include:

- *Networking through local sales and marketing clubs.* You'll not only make contacts with sales reps in a variety of industries, but also learn tips about marketing your own services.
- *Marketing your services through hotels and motels where traveling reps stay.* At convention hotels and other higher-priced hotels, you can contact the concierge to get referrals to sales reps who inquire about desktop design and publishing services. At motels and lower-cost hotels, ask if you can advertise your services on a bulletin board or leave cards for employees to distribute.
- *Offering fast, dependable, overnight service and delivery.* Sales reps may need overnight revisions on presentations or proposals. Being available after 5:00 P.M. weekdays, when most quick printers are closed, is one way to provide indispensable service.

swamped and need extra help to fill orders. And they may need help handling jobs that require special talent or services they don't offer.

Existing Clients: The Best Market of All

Finding new clients can mean plenty of hard work. The best way to lighten the load is by tapping your most valuable resource: the clients you already have. The cheapest, easiest ways to generate business are to keep the clients you get, increase their use of your services, and get them to spread the word about you.

Keeping the clients you get seems easy in principle. Do a good job at a fair price and they'll keep coming back. But as in any human relationship, it's a little more complex. Keeping clients happy involves many factors, both tangible and intangible. Here are some time-tested strategies:

- *Prevent unpleasant surprises.* Always give clients an estimate before a job starts, and stick to it when you bill. Clients' concepts of what a job will cost may be wildly unrealistic. An estimate will clear any doubts and keep you from having to defend a bill later. If the job takes longer because of mistakes you made, swallow the cost and mark it down as experience. If the job runs longer because of changes the client has made, let him or her know when the changes are suggested how they'll affect the final bill.
- *Ask questions relentlessly when taking a brief before work begins.* The time to clear up misunderstandings is before you invest time.
- *Outline a range of options for a job in terms of cost, style, etc.* When possible, show clients examples of what you have in mind before you start to work on it.
- *Don't be afraid to make suggestions that can improve a job.* But don't be overbearing about getting things done your way.
- *Practice self-improvement.* Read trade publications to get more familiar with what your clients do. Take workshops to constantly improve your skills.

■ *Deliver on time*. Bring in contractors if necessary to meet the deadline.

■ *Put your name on your work*. Then your clients will spread the word about you when they spread the word about themselves.

■ *Don't forget about clients after the job*. An occasional phone call, cards at holidays or client newsletters are good ways to keep your name in front of your clients.

■ *Make yourself indispensable*. Find ways to make your client's job easier by improving and expanding the services you provide. If you only handle design, take on more production, editorial or other aspects of projects, even if it means turning to outside contractors. Your ability to bring a team to a project gives your clients all the clout of an ad agency without all the cost.

■ *Keep a database file on every client, including dates of when work was performed*. Many clients and jobs work on a seasonal cycle, so you can anticipate when a project might repeat itself in coming quarters or years. Call up listings under the date field of your database monthly to get an idea of which projects start last year or last quarter and could be restarting soon. By calling a client well in advance of the job, you may jog her or his memory and make sure the job comes back to you.

Another way to keep clients coming back is to constantly increase and improve your services. For instance, if you've started outputting to film, that can speed your turnaround time; let clients know about this. Don't assume they know about all of the services you can offer.

Most successful businesses get their clients from word of mouth. That makes it seem like all you need to do is get a few clients and wait for the word to spread. But your initiative can make word of mouth work more effectively. Gently remind your customers to let their friends and associates know about you.

And ask your customers and acquaintances for references to potential clients they may know. Having a name to drop takes a lot of the chill off the eventual cold call. You may even offer clients a bounty — in the form of a percentage reduction in their bill — for every new client they steer your way.

Networking: The Ties That Bring in Business

Networking — that overworked buzzword of the eighties — is an unescapable necessity for marketing a desktop design and publishing business. As time-consuming and imprecise as it may be, it's still one of the cheapest and most effective marketing tools around. Networking won't land you business right away, and if you start trying to close deals over dinner at a club meeting or a party, you'll probably do yourself more harm than good. But networking is a great way to develop relationships that will lead to business in the long run.

Surprisingly, some of the best networking you can do is with your "competitors." Joining a local group of desktop designers and publishers is a great way not only to swap ideas about technique, but also to swap clients. Yours is a field dominated by solo practitioners and small shops. No matter how hard you try to manage your work load, you're eventually going to get swamped. A desktop design and publishing group, or a more informal network of colleagues, is the best way to find help. In turn, you can expect your colleagues to return the favor. As long as you're not aggressively stealing clients from them, you can expect a lot of cooperation. Sometimes this entails steering a client toward someone whose skills or experience better match her or his needs. A more-experienced, more-expensive desktop designer and publisher may refer a lower-budget account to someone just getting started. Or someone who has no experience in health care may want to refer a client to someone who does.

One warning: The clients you get through this channel may not always be a blessing. Some desktop designers and publishers slough off their problem clients this way. If their problem was a personality conflict, that may not be bad. But watch out for slow payers, bill hagglers and relentless revisers, all of whom result in your doing lots of work you never get paid for. Don't be afraid to look a gift horse in the mouth. Call to thank colleagues who refer work your way. But at the same time politely ask why they did.

The other networking channels you choose may require a little more enterprise. Sales and marketing clubs are one good route. So is any trade organization for an industry in which you specialize. Even if you don't qualify as a full member of the group, you may be allowed in as an associate member. Getting involved not only helps you meet potential clients, it also keeps you informed about issues in the industry that can help you serve them better.

Don't overlook local chambers of commerce, either. Most have monthly after-hours get-togethers for members to schmooze. You'll find a lot of people here trying to sell each other things. But since salespeople need your help as much if not more than anyone else, that can be a plus. Joining the chamber also gets you in and gives you access to a chamber directory, which is a great source of leads for potential clients and mailing lists. The chamber also may offer group health insurance and direct you to free business advice. And being a member helps you be taken seriously as a business person, particularly important for a home-based business.

Your computer opens even more paths for networking, especially if you have a modem. Local user groups can be a good way to meet computer-literate folks who can help you on the technical side and might need help on the design side. Local bulletin boards and national networks, such as CompuServe and Prodigy, can do two things: help you contact potential clients through user forums, and get you free software and advice on technical problems.

Publications to Monitor: Getting the Word on Prospects

A regular part of your marketing strategy should be monitoring key newspapers, newsletters and magazines. Not only do you develop leads this way, but you also keep up with trends that affect your clients' businesses and, ultimately, your own.

Your local daily newspaper is a good place to start. Looking beyond the front page, it's got a wealth of potential marketing information. The classifieds, for instance, are one of the best sources of leads, but not always in the ways you'd suspect. Look for ads seeking managers in sales, marketing, public relations, corporate communications and personnel. The people who end up taking these jobs may need to develop a network of contractors to help them. If they come from out of town, they're almost certain to be unfamiliar with the local market. But even if they rose through the ranks with a company, they may still be developing contacts with desktop designers and publishers for the first time. Even if their predecessor leaves them with a host of contacts, they may want to establish their independence by finding their own help.

Also look for ads from businesses that want full-time or part-time desktop designers and publishers. You may be able to talk them into using your services by stressing the cost savings on training, benefits and the lower overall overhead. If you can't handle all the work, you can give some to contractors and still provide more flexibility and lower overhead than an employee would give the company.

Some businesses advertise freelance desktop design and publishing jobs in the "Help Wanted" section. You can't find a hotter lead than that. Even though the competition for advertised work is heavy, such ads could lead to great clients for you.

Beyond the classifieds, use the business section to keep track of which businesses are growing—or laying off workers. A local business weekly will probably cover business developments in your area in greater depth than a daily. In either type of publication, things you should watch for include:

■ *Columns announcing promotions and new hires.* These may be good people to contact directly, or at least to keep on file for future contact.

■ *Announcements by advertising and public relations agencies of new accounts.* That could be a sign the agency will need freelance help.

■ *Calendars of club and association meetings and seminars.* You can attend these to network.

■ *Listings of new incorporations or vendor's licenses, which could provide leads on new businesses.* Keep in mind that not all new incorporations are new businesses. Some are just proprietorships or partnerships that changed their status. But checking in the phone book could

Taking Full Service to the Max

Thousands of printers started offering desktop design and publishing services in recent years, but seldom has the process worked the other way around. One exception is Designs n' Type, a Sunrise, Florida, full-service graphic arts and printing company, where the transition from desktop design and publishing to full-service printing has been a dramatic success.

Partners Brian Blanchette and Chuck Levine started the business in 1986 as B&C Computerized Typesetting. "All we did was desktop publishing," says Blanchette. "We brokered out our printing to a local printer and didn't say we were the printers. But the general public didn't care how a document was produced. They only wanted it to look nice and cost less. When we talked about desktop publishing, they turned their heads like a dog hearing a whistle. It was a great hindrance to explaining what we did."

So, a year after starting the business, Blanchette and Levine changed their name and their marketing approach. "We totally remarketed ourselves as a full-service graphic design and printing firm," Blanchette says. "And people understood that." When it first made the switch to full service, Designs n' Type was a printer only by virtue of brokering the printing. But by working eighty-hour weeks and plowing as much money as humanly possible into the business, the company bought an offset press. Now, Designs n' Type handles everything from printing wedding invitations to preparing corporate identity packages and computerizing mailing lists.

Years later, the tables have turned. People come in asking if Designs n' Type does desktop design and publishing. Now their job is to set themselves apart from other printers who offer desktop design and publishing services, Blanchette says. "We don't push the fact that we do desk-

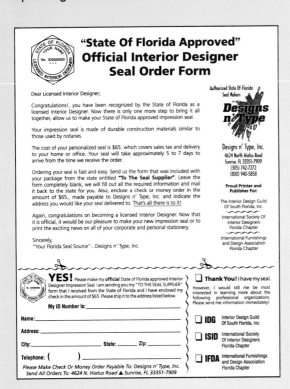

Designs n' Type, Sunrise, Florida, uses a full range of marketing materials to keep its name in front of clients and display the wide variety of work it can provide. Included in its marketing arsenal are Rolodex cards, an "Information and Value Pak" with coupons and discount information, letterhead that states the full range of services the company provides and an order form directed specifically at the interior design trade. (See pages 64-65.)

top publishing—only that it's quality. So many of these quick printers have hurt the industry by giving their services away and producing unprofessional documents by some school kid they're paying $5 an hour."

"My first love was and is desktop publishing," Blanchette says. "And that's still what we're strong in. We have state-of-the-art 486s and Linotronic equipment, and the printing takes a backseat to the preparation work."

Offering full service, however, provides numerous entry points for new customers, who can then be sold on other Designs n' Type services. The way Designs n' Type has built a huge client base in the interior design industry is a classic example of how it maximizes business from each client. "One of our first major clients was an interior designer, and a couple of others soon followed suit through word of mouth," Blanchette says. "When interior designers started being licensed by the state of Florida, we started manufacturing the license seals, which are like notary seals and are required

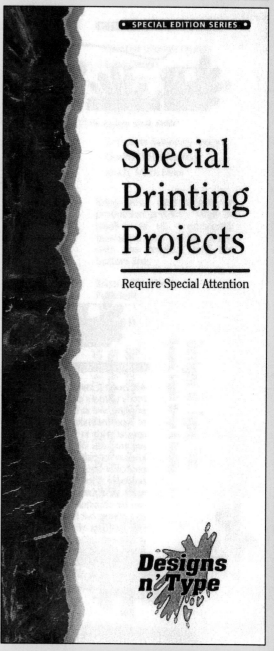

Full Service
Graphic Arts
& Printing

Newsletters
Letterheads
Envelopes
Logos
Business Cards
Doorhangers
Rolodex Cards
Postcards
Menus
Flyers
Brochures
Résumés
Catalogs
Directories
Labels
Estimates
Proposals
Term Papers
Mail Lists
Rubber Stamps
Invitations
Notices
NCR Forms
Invoices
Graphics
Typesetting
Scanning
Continuous Forms
Signs
Laser Printing
Desktop Publishing
Training
Consulting
Data Entry
Statements
Certificates
Coupons
Bumper Stickers
Letters
Bulk Mailing
Facsimile Services
Foil Stamping
Die Cutting
Perforating
Computers
Copies
Advertisements
Much, Much More!

Designs n' Type, Incorporated
4624 N. Hiatus Road ▲ Sunrise, Florida 33351-7909
(305) 742-7272 ▲ (800) 940-5858 ▲ Fax (305) 742-7219

by the state." As one of two companies in South Florida that makes the seals, Designs n' Type has developed a strong position with new interior designers. After getting names and addresses of new interior designers from the state, the company sends a mailing aimed not only at getting an order for seals, but also for a wide range of promotional materials. The company has amassed a mailing list of 5,000 interior designers in Florida. And besides working for many individual interior design-

ers and companies, Designs n' Type handles design and printing for three industry organizations.

The company also has hired two full-time sales reps and developed a network of designers, desktop publishers and quick printers who broker work and receive discounts off consumer rates. More recently, Designs n' Type branched into service bureau work, since few service bureaus are nearby. All of this led to expansion into a 2,600-square-foot office/warehouse in 1991.

tell you if the company existed previously.

■ *Listings of companies with tax liens, mechanic's liens and lawsuits for nonpayment and bankruptcy, which could keep you from getting stiffed.*

Of course, you should also get beyond the back-page listings to look for stories on companies and executives who could be potential clients.

If you've already developed a niche working with a particular industry or plan to target one, look for trade magazines and journals that cover the industry. Even if you don't subscribe to them, you may be able to scan them periodically at your library. You're unlikely to come across any information that could directly lead to a new client; but you will learn about industry issues, product development, terminology, and approaches taken by designers in trade ads. All these things can help you win new clients and serve the ones you have better.

To the extent possible, read the *Wall Street Journal* and major business magazines, such as *Fortune*, *Forbes* and *Business Week*. You don't need to get bogged down in the minutiae of securities trading, but you can keep up with trends in advertising, marketing and business presentations that affect your business. When these publications begin talking up things like multimedia presentations, you can bet it will have a profound influence on your clients and your business. Also, *Advertising Age*, *Adweek* and *Adweek's Marketing Week* can keep you abreast of developments that affect many areas of your business and your clients' business.

Using Your Computer to Market Yourself

Your most powerful marketing tools are your computer and your ability to use it effectively. They'd better be—because these are the same tools you're selling to clients. Making promotional materials is the most important marketing use for your computer. You're the first and most important customer you'll ever have for desktop design and publishing. Many desktop designers and publishers have résumés, brochures, business cards and letterhead they've

created for their businesses, in addition to their portfolios. But you can go far beyond those basic tools to create a package that helps polish your image and attract new business. Your identity package can include memo pads, invoices, statements, estimate forms, model contracts and more. The better designed *and* more complete the package, the more professional you look. Plus, showing clients creative products you've made for yourself gives them ideas for ways to use your services.

The computer can be a good way to quickly match your portfolio to a prospective client. The fact that you haven't had any clients for business forms or magazine design doesn't mean you can't have samples of each. True, it's much better to develop work samples for someone who's paying the bill. But doing a sample "on spec" may be the key to getting an important client. And, if nothing else, you can keep it as a template to start from when a similar job comes along.

Making Direct Mail Work

Desktop computers have made direct mail seem deceptively easy. And many desktop designers and publishers have found clients effectively by using direct mail. But probably far more have been disappointed with the results. That's because direct mail is an often-misused tool for small service businesses like yours. The problem isn't so much medium as method.

At best, direct mail is part of a strategy rather than a strategy in itself. It's not a substitute for personal client contact, but it can be a useful supplement. Unlike a mass merchandiser, you can't rely on huge numbers to make direct mail work. Not only will the costs of an indiscriminate mailing be prohibitive, but the effort required to make such a mailing work is beyond what a small operation can deliver. Few desktop designers and publishers report success with mailings larger than one hundred. Mailings even smaller than that can be quite successful if you've chosen your targets well.

A good rule to follow is never to send more mailings than you can follow up with a phone call in the following weeks. The personal touch is essential to making your mailing stand out from the daily pile of junk heaped on every business person's desk. The personal touch is even more important because you're selling a service, and the person who delivers news of that service is essential to the client's decision. Clients are likely to equate the level of attention they receive from you in the marketing phase with what they can expect from you later.

Rather than shipping out mailings randomly, target your mailings to specific industries or areas where your strengths lie. Gather the names from the sources discussed earlier in this chapter. You can supplement your list by using information from chamber of commerce directories or industrial directories carried in the public library, which have companies categorized according to their Standard Industrial Classification (SIC) Code. Clubs and trade or-

Direct-mail pieces range from the simple to the complex. This oversized postcard mailer does the job for Select Mail, Inc.

A simple brochure tells Sharon Sittner's clients about the services she can provide.

ganizations issue directories that also can be good resources. And magazines or trade journals may also have mailing lists available. If they're not willing to sell listings broken down by Zip Code or state, however, they'll probably be too expensive to use.

To manage a mailing, you can use one of the many commercially available database programs with mailing list management functions. Each time you discover a potential contact or prospect, enter it into your database for future mailings. You also can code entries according to industry or other category to tailor specialized mailings.

Tailoring your mailings to a select group lets you put more money into the quality of your mailing rather than fruitlessly mailing a low-budget flier to thousands of people. The expense of printing and mailing creates a strong temptation to cut corners on the direct-mail packages you send. But ultimately, that defeats the purpose. The impression you make with your own promotional material is of paramount importance.

What you mail usually affects the results in another way, too. Newsletters beget newsletter accounts. Brochures beget brochure jobs. You may get the best results by tailoring the contents of each direct-mail package to the kind of work you expect each client to need. If the prospective account is large enough, it may even be worthwhile to create a package specifically for the client, including a prototype of a newsletter or brochure.

Though the design of your package is crucial, you shouldn't short shrift the copywriting. It will pay to have a copywriter or advertising professional write your copy and help develop the concept to make sure it works. You might try exchanging your design for a writer's copy in developing promotional material for both. If you plan on having a long-term working relationship with the writer, you might even create a joint marketing piece and share mailing costs. Bringing illustrators, photographers and other related professionals on board may further enhance the piece and its impact.

No matter how good the package you mail, it won't get you far without a follow-up call. Direct mail—even good direct mail—tends to

Personal Touch Makes Marketing Work

If talent alone could guarantee success, Chicago's Feldman/Narayan Inc. would never have to lift a finger to get clients. During their first year in business, partners Mark Feldman and Lakshmi Narayan won a host of awards for their work, including the grand prize in *Publish* magazine's 1991 Design Awards. But building their business has meant considerable planning, mailing and legwork rather than waiting for reputation to bring customers through their door.

"The awards don't have a lot of impact on clients themselves," Feldman says. "They want to know what you're going to do for them, whether you're going to solve their problems and do it within their budget." The award provided the fledgling studio with a new set of fonts and a strong reputation in the design community, but they still had to work hard to get clients.

Feldman and Narayan were fortunate to start with one major client—Evangelical Health Systems, their former employer for whom they created the piece that won the *Publish* award. The two worked so well together there for three years that they decided to start their own business.

The bulk of Feldman and Narayan's marketing has been through a combination of mailings and telephone follow-ups. They used listings of top public and private companies in a local business weekly to get names of potential clients. Then they called the companies to identify the executives in marketing, advertising and personnel departments who might use

be put aside. The only way to get it—and you—back to the front of the client's mind is to call. You'll likely get rejected, but even if you only get a positive response for one of ten mailings, you're ahead of the game. Even a one in one hundred success rate can be worthwhile if it generates a long-term, high-paying account.

design services. Their research yielded about one hundred prospective clients. They sent a mailing that included a sample of four transparencies of their work on a black mount, a promotional letter and business cards—all of which fit in regular No. 10 envelopes. In following weeks, they made phone calls to their prospects. Subsequent mailings were smaller and targeted particular industries, such as health care, manufacturers and real estate companies, but otherwise followed the same format.

"We got good response," Feldman says. "About 90 percent of the people we mailed to remembered us when we called." But getting meetings was a little tougher. About twenty-five of the first one hundred prospects agreed to a meeting. And ultimately, that early effort yielded two clients. Considering the economic climate at the time, Feldman considers the mailings a success. And the groundwork laid with that initial mailing remains in place. "Most of the people who we initially contacted, we've continued following up with," Feldman says. "Many of them asked us to call and send future examples of our work."

Follow-up is the key to making a mailing work, he says. "If we hadn't followed up, we wouldn't have gotten any responses at all. It's got to be linked to that personal contact, because people get so much junk mail." Feldman and Narayan plan to continue sending simpler promotional mailings to prospects contacted in the early rounds of marketing.

One goal of their marketing is to get beyond reliance on the health-care industry, where their considerable experience has already given them a strong client base. "We don't want to be pigeonholed into one industry," Feldman says.

"We feel like if we have a variety of clients—some in industry, some in real estate, some in retailing—we can better weather the ups and downs of the economy."

So far, the studio has picked up new clients in real estate and diversified its health-care clientele by doing work for pharmaceutical companies. "It's a slow process that takes a lot of patience and persistence," he says. "You have to tailor your portfolio so when you go into a meeting, you're not showing all health care to a client."

Even so, some clients are hard to sell when a designer doesn't have experience in their industry. Feldman and Narayan stress that even though each industry has its own nuances, a designer's ability to solve design problems and communicate to diverse audiences are the key skills needed. "I got one real estate investment company executive on the phone and told who I was and what I do," Feldman says. "He asked flatly whether we've done any real estate brochures before, and I had to tell him no. I said while I could see where he was coming from, that if you only go to designers who've done that kind of thing before, you're likely to get a pretty common product rather than fresh insight." That got Feldman and Narayan as far as a presentation meeting and proposal, but the job ultimately went to a designer with real estate experience.

The designers also attend monthly meetings of a local Young Executives Club to make contacts and circulate business cards. While they're comfortable with marketing themselves, they've found it takes away from their time to serve clients. In the long run, the partners hope to hire a commissioned sales rep to expand their business.

Advertising: Finding Low-Cost, High-Impact Media

Few desktop designers and publishers advertise, and for good reason: It often doesn't work. Conventional advertising works best for larger businesses that can afford to spend the money and take the time to make a lasting impression. Other marketing approaches, such as networking, are a lot cheaper. And direct mail gives you

the power to focus efforts on the clients you really want.

But there are some relatively low-cost, high-impact media that can work for you. The Yellow Pages is a key example. Having an ad listing in the Yellow Pages helps establish you as a serious business. That's all the more important for the vast number of desktop designers and publishers who run their businesses from their homes. The Yellow Pages also works in harmony with other marketing strategies. Your other promotional efforts may have planted your name in a prospective client's mind only vaguely; your Yellow Pages ad can jog a fuzzy memory and lead to a sale. Though a Yellow Pages ad is less expensive than many other forms of advertising, it's still not cheap. It will cost a few hundred dollars per year.

Advertising in a local newspaper will usually reach a general audience, most of which won't need your services. Thus, it's usually a waste of money. One exception is classified advertising to target specific consumer markets—such as an ad near the "Help Wanted" section for résumé services. Local business weeklies or monthlies offer a more focused market and usually a better deal. The advantage is that you're reaching the corporate and small-business audiences you want in the region you want rather than paying for circulation you don't need. Some business papers offer business-card-size ads or service directory listings that are inexpensive enough for you to maintain year-round placement.

Evaluate how effective your advertising is. One way is by using coupons or simply asking people who call how they heard about you. Keep a record of your contacts from various ads and other marketing approaches to find what's most cost effective. Don't forget to track the billings from clients who've come from different marketing methods, since that rather than sheer numbers through the door is the best yardstick of what your marketing efforts yield.

Conventions and Trade Shows

Exhibiting at conventions and trade shows can be a good way to meet potential clients. But it's a costly route. Besides the booth fee, you also need time and money to build and tend the booth. Considering the costs, you should only consider exhibiting at shows if:

- They're narrowly focused on the printing or graphics trade, so that they'll bring in attendees interested in your services.
- You're acquainted with the management from attending past events and know the

Aggressive Marketing Builds Desktop Publishing Business

Lynne Perry used a combination of creative marketing, fast service and diversity to get her desktop publishing and computer support business off to a fast start in 1990. Her novel marketing approach avoids staples such as advertising and direct marketing in favor of free samples, customer referral incentives and pro bono work. Along the way, she tried more traditional approaches and more offbeat approaches that failed.

Advertising in a local newspaper brought Perry's business, Lyn.Sys, little response. So did her direct mailing to about 400 businesses culled from the Yellow Pages in her hometown of Rochester, New York. She even tried cold calling businesses looking for clerical help in the "Help Wanted" ads, figuring she could sell them on her broad-based computer services instead. She couldn't. "Cold calling for DTP just doesn't work in this area," she says. "There are too many printers, and too many of them offer desktop publishing services."

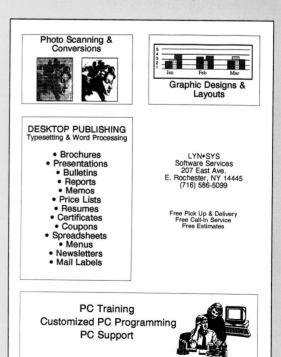

Photo Scanning & Conversions

Graphic Designs & Layouts

DESKTOP PUBLISHING
Typesetting & Word Processing

- Brochures
- Presentations
- Bulletins
- Reports
- Memos
- Price Lists
- Resumes
- Certificates
- Coupons
- Spreadsheets
- Menus
- Newsletters
- Mail Labels

LYN•SYS
Software Services
207 East Ave.
E. Rochester, NY 14445
(716) 586-5099

Free Pick Up & Delivery
Free Call-In Service
Free Estimates

PC Training
Customized PC Programming
PC Support

Thwarted in early attempts to sell her work, she started giving it away as a promotion. Perry wrestled with how to convince clients she could produce a better publication for them than what they were already doing themselves without wounding their vanity. Her answer was to do sample publications and send them to target businesses, who could use them for free as long as they used them unaltered. Since the publications carried a line plugging Lyn.Sys, they provided advertising for her even if they didn't win her that particular client.

Perry also enclosed a letter telling the prospective clients she'd like their business in the future, and then followed up with the phone call asking if they used the sample and, if not, how she could improve it so they would. The approach yielded four clients from ten attempts and a total investment of twelve hours.

Doing free publications for charities and fundraising events was another route Perry used to get free advertising. In return for doing the publication, she receives ad space for her business. That gives her automatic circulation to members of what's often a tight-knit group whose members patronize each others' businesses, she says.

With clients generated through such "investment marketing," Perry began working on word-of-mouth advertising and increasing sales through existing clients. She publishes a one-page quarterly newsletter for clients to keep her name in their minds, introduce them to new services she offers, and encourage referrals. To give clients an incentive to recommend Lyn.Sys, Perry offers a 15 percent rebate on billings for the previous quarter for any client whose referral leads to a new client. Overall, such tactics have required relatively little investment of time and gives clients a sense of being partners, Perry says.

Speed and breadth of service has also been an important part of winning clients, Perry says. One client, a sales manager whose business encompasses the East Coast, turns to Perry when he needs sales materials overnight before trips. Another client, a career consultant, uses Lyn.Sys for overnight résumés. To accommodate such clients, she maintains daily hours of noon to 9:00 P.M.

Lynne Perry's approach in marketing materials is to offer clients a variety of services and a better understanding of the types of services she can provide.

DeskTop Publishing (commonly referred to as DTP) is a computerized process used to produce a wide variety of quality documentation.

Much of the confusion people experience upon first exposures to the term is due to the vast capabilities of DeskTop Publishers. One person may see DTP as a word processing or typing process, while another sees it as a graphic artists or illustrators tool. Still a third person may define it as the actual high quality printed output. All are correct. DTP simultaneously replaces typewriters, mechanical layouts, hand produced illustrations, offset printers and typesetters, and to some degree even calculators and photographers.

One of the fastest growing technologies in the computer arena, more and more business is turning to DeskTop Publishing to produce their documentation, and for good reasons!

COMMONLY USED DTP TERMS

Clip Art	- purchased 'general use' illustrations & pictures
DPI	- Dots per inch, used in referring to print density. The higher quality of print contains more DPI.
Font	- refers to the Typeface of printable characters.
Graphic	- a visual representation or illustration.
Page Maker	- the software used to compose a documents text and/or graphic placements.
Paint	- computer Freehand drawing abilities
Paste	- to move or insert text or graphics into a computer document
Scale	- to resize an object in a document
Scan	- to convert an image such as a photograph to a digitized computer readable image.
Spell Checker	- a software tool used to electronically search for spelling errors
Word Processor	- a software tool used to input text to a computer.

Quality

Business today is finding that the need to provide improved presentation through their documentation is critical to maintaining a competitive edge in their respective marketing industries. With DTP, even a simple document, such as an office memo, takes on a highly professional appearance.

Speed

The DeskTop Publisher has all the tools needed to produce a document in one central location (the computer), and documents which at one time took days or weeks are now being produced in hours! For example, *this brochure* was conceived, developed, and produced in less than 8 hours!

Versatility

All aspects of a document layout can be incorporated for output by DeskTop Publishers, from the actual text copy and photo images to computer generated spread sheets, graphs and illustrations. Whether the document is a simple brochure or a fully illustrated technical manual, DTP is the only process flexible enough to allow multiple imaging control.

Performance

With the use of spelling and grammer verifiers, errors are substantially reduced. Design changes are effected with ease as their impact to other areas of the document are usually minimal. Adjustments and corrections are made quickly, with the final results available for proofing almost instantly.

Cost

Few businesses require full time publishing personnel, and most find it impractical to invest in DTP on a part time basis. Many businesses are finding that using a DTP service is the most cost effective means of producing quality documentation without the added burden of personnel, payroll, and equipment.

show will be well promoted and attended.

- You can find a way to demonstrate why you're different and better than other desktop designers and publishers who will exhibit at the show.
- You develop a way to get the names, addresses and phone numbers of people who come by your booth for future reference. Using a giveaway drawing is one approach.

Pro Bono Work

Desktop designers and publishers, like all professionals, have an aversion to giving away their work. But there are two strong arguments to donate your work to charity. One, it's for a good cause. Two, it can generate free advertising, goodwill and clients. The good cause part is a matter of looking into your own heart and wallet. But the second part is strictly business sense. Doing free design work for charities and fundraising events puts you in good stead with members of the organization, who may then recommend you to their friends. In many cases, the folks sitting on charity boards are business leaders whose influence on your behalf could be very valuable. Also, you may be able to arrange free advertising in any promotional piece you create. That gives you free distribution of your "ad" in a prestigious publication.

Cold Calls

With luck, networking and positive word of mouth, you can avoid cold calls. But expanding into new areas or starting a new business almost always involves a little cold calling. Preceding your call with a mailing and having as much information as possible on the prospective cli-

ent takes much of the chill off. Here are some other ways to make the cold call easier to face:

- *Use the phone.* In most cases, that's the best way to initiate personal contact. Even if it's important to show your portfolio, the only way in the door is usually an appointment made by phone. Getting past secretaries can be hard, even on the phone. If your best efforts are thwarted, try calling before 9:00 A.M. or after 5:00 P.M., when secretaries may be gone and it's easier to make contact directly. One exception to phoning first may be when you approach storefront businesses. Provided you stop by when it's not busy and you don't stay long, a personal visit won't seem like an intrusion.
- *Plan what you're going to say.* Don't do a hard sell or sound like a hyperactive telemarketer with a five-minute spiel. But do—after introducing yourself—provide a one- or two-sentence description of who you are and what you have to offer.
- *If you sent a direct mailing, ask if the person received it and if he or she might be interested in your services some time in the future.* Even if the answer is no, ask if you can check back in a few months. Or you can ask if the person knows of anyone else who might need your services.
- *Be honest.* Don't use gimmicks, such as saying you're conducting a survey about usage of desktop design and publishing. People can see through such ruses and resent being used. If you truly are seeking market research information, however, be forthright about who you are and why you're doing the survey.
- *If the prospect is using someone else, ask for an opportunity to prepare a no-obligation bid on a future job.*

Escape from New York Brings Two-City Business

Eric Otto had a successful design partnership in New York City, but he longed to get away from the city's daily hassles. His answer was to leave New York in 1990 and set up a new studio—Terrapin Design—in Charlotte, North Carolina. He selected Charlotte because of its climate and its status as a regional financial center. That seemed perfectly suited to Otto's background as a former art director with the New York investment bank Shearson Lehman Hutton. But setting up shop in a new place has been a lot like starting a business from scratch, Otto says. In the process, he's learned some hard-knock marketing lessons.

"The first group I went after were existing studios and advertising agencies, figuring they already had clients," he says. "I know the business well enough to know that the work load varies, and there's no way to match your production capacity to the number of people coming in your door." Otto contacted art directors by mail and phone, then arranged personal interviews. The agencies and studios were Otto's first and best marketing targets. "Most people, when they saw my résumé, were very interested if they had work along the corporate line. In some cases, I'm called just because they need extra bodies. And I've worked for a couple of studios who have no desktop publishing capability at all and, surprisingly, don't want to get into it." Work for studios and agencies helped expose Otto to other corporate accounts through word of mouth, which now accounts for most of his new business.

Otto also tried direct mailings to prospective clients, but mostly with disappointing results. Though letters to studios, agencies and printers produced results, a second mailing to 400 prospective business clients yielded no responses. "One disadvantage to coming into the city blind is that I don't know where the market is, so I'm taking kind of a shotgun approach," he says. He joined the chamber of commerce and used its directory as his principal mailing list. But without personal knowledge of the businesses and whom to contact, he was left to rely on the mailer alone without follow-up. "It wasn't an exceptionally good mailer, either," he says. "It was one-color with cheap paper." And while the brochure had extensive copy telling executives why they shouldn't rely on their secretaries to do their design work, it gave short shrift to why Terrapin Design was a better alternative.

In a second mailing, Otto refined his approach. The four-color card focuses on Otto's background and services, stressing value, versatility and design skill. Otto also refined his mailing list by getting names and titles from business publications and wedding announcements. And he's broadened personal contacts with prospective clients by attending chamber get-togethers. The result has been several responses he hopes to turn into long-lasting clients.

Meanwhile, Otto has kept in touch with clients in New York and proved that—with modern technology—a desktop designer and publisher can be in two places at the same time. "Not being in New York physically, I can't do any real marketing," he says. But many clients have stayed with him because they're comfortable with his work and see no reason to look elsewhere. Otto maintains a New York phone number that he checks several times a day so he can return calls promptly. "Without the computer, modem and fax, it wouldn't work," he says. "But because the technology is there, I've been able to hold onto most of my New York clients."

Though Otto hasn't lowered his hourly rate, he's discovered he can service New York accounts more efficiently from Charlotte than from New York. "If you're physically there in the city, people will demand you come over in person, and you have to bill them for that if you're going to make any money. Having 700 miles between you means you can't just drop by the office, and I don't bill them for faxes and phone calls."

Eric Otto found his first mailer for Terrapin Design in Charlotte, North Carolina, was a good concept, but too wordy and ultimately ineffective.

Before you ask your secretary* to take care of your design problems, think about this...

*or your administrative assistant, husband, wife, boyfriend, girlfriend, anyfriend, significant other, casual acquaintance or yourself...

Your image is vitally important to your business. The printed materials you produce and distribute are a snapshot of your company. They tell your customers and clients how well your business is run and how much pride you take in the goods and services you provide. You expect a high level of professionalism in your employees and representatives, and your printed materials should reflect the same professional attitude.

So before you blithely hand off your graphic design problems to the first willing and available person, here are three good reasons to reconsider:

1. Your secretary is not a graphic designer. Intelligent, well organized, efficient, talented and hard working, yes. But graphic design is more than running a few paragraphs through the dot matrix printer and slapping in some clip-art. There are dozens and dozens of unseen pitfalls between an idea and a final printed page that can unnecessarily run up your costs.

As the owner of Terrapin Design, Mr. Eric Otto represents over fifteen years of design and production experience in the toughest market in the country. In addition, Terrapin draws on the talents and expertise of affiliated specialists to ensure that your graphic design program is appropriate and memorable as well as affordable. Our low overhead and extensive use of computerized production makes substantial savings possible for our clients.

2. Your secretary does not have the equipment. They call them "microcomputers," but there is nothing micro about the cost. In order to reap the cost benefits from the "desktop publishing" revolution you need to invest in excess of $10,000– possibly as much as $25,000. And first cost is never final cost.

So don't count on your Mac Plus or your IBM clone to give you great results. With each new update and new release, today's graphics programs have turned into memory hogs. The older and smaller systems simply do not have the speed or the muscle to handle the state-of-the-art programming.

Terrapin Design has already made the investment for you. We have the equipment that has the speed and muscle, and the up-to-date programs to give you the cost-effective graphic design and production that you need.

3. Your secretary does not have the time. If she did, you probably don't really need a secretary. Graphic design is not something you pick up overnight. It takes years of experience just to get a feel for the industry, and a good design is not something you doodle on a napkin at lunchtime. If its to be done right, the best investment you can make is time.

The same is true for desktop production. The days of "intuitive" training are long gone as the newer programs continue to add a dizzying array of features and capabilities. Learning curves are getting steeper and steeper, and it could be weeks or months from the time you load a program until you see some truly gratifying results. And time spent on training is time lost on other duties and responsibilities.

At Terrapin, we've been up to speed since before day one. Our experience with computerized graphics goes back beyond the first Macintosh to the days of the Apple LISA, the forerunner of today's Macintosh desktop publishing systems.

And when it comes to time, we won't waste yours. We'll be there when you need us, and the rest of the time we will be diligently, if silently, working to give you the quality graphic design you need within the budget you have.

On the other hand... you can spend tens of thousands of dollars on equipment and software, you can send your secretary away to art school for four years, and when she gets back you can hire an assistant to take over all of her other duties while she turns her attention to your graphic design problems.

Or you can call Terrapin Design.

TERRAPIN

Eric P. Otto
President

704 556 1677

Graphic design,
photography and
microcomputer
production for
communications
and marketing

• Fill in the card below, detach and mail •

Please give me a call!

I am interested in discussing the following:

❑ Newsletters
❑ Brochures
❑ Logo / Corporate Identity
❑ Catalogs / Price Lists / Forms
❑ Advertising / Flyers / Direct Mail
❑ Publications / Reports
❑ Promotions
❑ Other: _____
_____
_____

Name: _____

Company: _____

Title: _____

Address: _____

City: _____

State / Zip: _____

Telephone: _____

Best Time To Call: _____

TERRAPIN DESIGN

He turned to a simpler approach the second time around with better results.

We believe the investment you make in your marketing, communications and company image is one of the most important investments you can make.

We believe you deserve to get the most value you can for that investment.

We believe you should talk to us before you invest another dime.

What We Do...

We design, illustrate and typeset the printed materials you need for your business.

Terrapin Design is committed to helping you develop, polish and preserve your professional image. We can help you establish an identity and advertise your products and services. We can produce the forms you need to conduct your business, reduce your paperwork and boost your efficiency. We can design and illustrate reports that are readable and technical manuals that instruct instead of confuse. We can give you Annual Reports that inform, brochures that sell and flyers that put out the word.

Best of all, we can put more of your budget to work on meeting your graphic design and typesetting needs and less into meeting our overhead.

Who We Are...

Terrapin Design was created in 1990 when its owner, Mr. Eric P. Otto, moved away from New York City in favor of Charlotte's less threatening environment. During his fifteen years in New York, Mr. Otto served as a production editor with Plenum Publishing, as an art director with Shearson Lehman Hutton, and as a general partner with KO Studio. During this time he mastered a number of commercial design and production techniques, including use of the Compugraphics Quadex and AdVantage II, Xyvision layout systems, the Apple LISA and the Macintosh IIx.

In addition to Charlotte, Terrapin Design draws on associated and affiliated talents and resources from across the country to ensure that you get the most value for your graphic design investment.

TERRAPIN
DESIGN

704/556-1677

8535 Winter Oaks Lane
Suite 102
Charlotte, NC 28210

Graphic Design

Brochures
Flyers
Print Advertising
Newsletters
Company Identity
Annual Reports
Logos
Charts/Slides
Technical Reports
Manuals
Price Lists
Catalogs

Data Handling

DOS-Mac Translations
Mac-Mac Translations
Text and Graphic
  Scanning

Tech Support

Training: Page Layout,
  Draw, and Paint
  programs
System and File
  Management

Positioning Your Business for Success

Ultimately, the key to making any marketing strategy work is what you're marketing. Not only do your skills and value have to measure up, but you need to let prospective clients know why they should turn to you rather than another desktop designer and publisher, full-service printer, or secretary with a desktop computer. Just being able to use a computer isn't enough in an increasingly competitive market. Here are some ways to stand above the competition:

■ *Skill*. Anybody with enough money can buy a computer and a few programs, but they're only tools whose value rests with the people who use them. Your experience and artistic skill can make you stand apart from the rest.

■ *Value*. Billing yourself as the lowest-cost desktop designer and publisher in town is usually a no-win strategy. Even if you get clients, you'll end up working for such low rates that you'd wish you hadn't. Being the highest *or* lowest bidder isn't the best position. Ideally, you can be somewhere in the middle but offer clients the same service and talent as the highest-priced alternative. Highlighting value—the ratio of quality/service to price—can be a strong selling point.

■ *Full service*. One way to stand apart from your competitors is to offer related services of copywriting, photography, illustration and mailing services. Through your diverse background or network of affiliated professionals, you can offer the convenience of one-stop shopping without the hefty price tag of an ad agency and consulting services.

■ *Speed*. Offering overnight service is one way to separate yourself from the competition. Asking for a premium—such as 25 percent to 33 percent—isn't unreasonable. But you might waive the premium for new clients (or if you're a new business that needs the work).

■ *Specialization*. Your background with clients in health care, financial services or other well-defined industries can help develop your reputation in the entire industry.

■ *Technical prowess*. Special expertise and equipment in areas such as color image editing or electronic darkroom work could be your ticket to winning high-end accounts.

Chapter Four

The Business Side

Computer skills and effective marketing are only part of the formula for success. How well you organize your business and navigate difficult tax and legal channels are just as important. There's no magic formula for taking care of business matters. But your business is much more likely to prosper if you:

- Develop a business plan
- Work out a competitive pricing structure
- Consider the tax consequences of your decisions
- Find simple ways to protect yourself legally

How Do I Know I'll Make Money?

As previous chapters have shown, the options for making money with a desktop computer are almost endless—so endless, they can be confusing. There's no better way to cut through that confusion than with a business plan. A business plan basically outlines the conditions your business faces and your strategy for thriving within those conditions. It's like a comp that leads the way to the finely tuned camera-ready mechanical that will become your business. It's also like a brief you present to a client to outline needs, goals and deadlines. Only you're the client, and the brief tells how you can best serve yourself.

Even if you're adding a desktop computer to an existing business, it can change things so much that it forces you to adjust your current strategy. A business plan can help you do that. Fortunately, the computer is a great tool for drafting your plan. You can use your standard word processing, spreadsheet and desktop design and publishing software, or software tailored specifically for business plans.

Business plans are important. But you don't need a 500-page spiral-bound plan with four-color graphics prepared by a Harvard M.B.A. You *do* need something that analyzes your market and how you plan to operate in it. Provided you don't have to show the plan to anyone, it can be as informal as a notebook full of notes. "Business plan," unfortunately, is a phrase that makes artists' eyes glaze over. But not doing a business plan can get you into trouble. Without some kind of plan, you may not anticipate all the costs that lay ahead or grasp all the opportunities that come along.

You may have met successful desktop designers and publishers who've never had a formal business plan. This may even be a good sign. A business plan is often a tool for getting loans, so not having one may be a sign that they didn't have to saddle their business with debt at the outset.

Some new businesses, on the other hand, may create elaborate business plans but never actually do much business. This may be the sign of someone who's in love with the idea of being in business but not with the hard work of actually running one. I knew one would-be desktop designer and publisher who drew up a business plan with an elaborate budget and even incorporated the business. But she didn't have a single client or solid prospect lined up. Not even a business plan could keep her in operation more than a few months.

So what's the point in drawing up a business plan? Here are several:

1. If you need to get a bank loan for your computer equipment or your business, you must show the bank your business plan. How professional the plan looks and, more important, how feasible it seems, can play a big part in getting the loan. If your business doesn't have much of a track record, the plan is the most important information a bank has to judge your credit-worthiness.

2. Even if you don't need a business loan, a business plan could help you get a personal loan. The self-employed can find home mortgages very difficult to get, especially if they've been in business less than two years. A home-based business may look suspect to conservative loan officers. But showing the loan officer a plan can help demonstrate that your business is serious. The more professional the plan looks and reads, the more convincing it will be.

3. A plan can help you decide whether your business idea will work. It takes you through steps such as analyzing your potential client base, competition and strategy. It makes you estimate expenses and income. And it can give you an idea of how long it will be until you make money.

4. If you're already in business, the plan can help you analyze what you're doing. It can show you what's most profitable or what part of your business is growing the fastest. If you're adding new equipment, the plan can help you evaluate how the equipment will affect your business, how long it will take to recoup your investment, or how you should adjust your fees to account for the improved productivity.

5. A plan can help spell out agreements between partners or inform employees of the company's goals. If one partner is primarily a designer and another is primarily a sales rep and business manager, the plan spells out the duties of each. For employees, the plan may provide a vision of what you want to do far more completely than anything you say.

6. Business plans also force you to consider external factors. By requiring you to analyze the competition, the plan makes you think about why you're different and better; once you have a firm idea of why you're better, you can explain that to potential clients more easily. By making you consider the economic factors of your industry and locality, the plan prepares you to adapt to the future.

How To Write A Business Plan

Business plans come in many sizes, and longer is not necessarily better. Your plan will have done its job if it clearly states:

1. Who you are
2. What you do
3. What your market is like
4. What your marketing and business strategy is
5. Whether you'll make money

Part One: Who Are You? (Company and Management Analysis)
Here are the elements of your company and management analysis:

- The legal name of your business
- Where it's located
- Its legal status, i.e., corporation, partnership or proprietorship
- A résumé of each principal owner,

operator or manager
- A history and description of the business
- The business' goals, both short- and long-term
- How many employees or partners the business will have and what their roles will be
- A listing and brief description of any key outside professionals or vendors you plan to use, such as accountants, business consultants, lawyers, designers, copywriters, photographers, etc.

Larger companies may separate the company and management analysis into different sections: One section analyzes the company using the above categories, another describes the backgrounds and roles of owners and managers. For one- and two-person operations, those two aspects are so intertwined that they should be combined.

Part Two: What Do You Do? (Service Analysis)
This is the crux of your plan and your business. It tells the reader:

- *Exactly which services or products you provide.*
- *Why they're different from and better than what's already out there.* For instance, you may have years of specialized experience designing brochures, annual reports and other collateral material for health-care providers. Or you may be able to undercut fees or improve turnaround time compared to larger design studios in your area.
- *How you plan to provide services.* Will you do all the work yourself? Will you farm some work out to a network of contractors? Also, you should have a description of your computer equipment, its advantages and capabilities, and your expertise with it.
- *Your location.* Do you have a home office in the suburbs or a downtown studio? How does your location affect your service? Is it near potential clients? Does it provide meeting space? How much is your rent? If you're in a home office, what percentage of your square footage does it take up, and what percentage is that of your housing costs?
- *Possible avenues of expansion.* If you do

newsletters now, will it make sense to do annual reports in a few years? What are some fast-growing or future markets that you can serve?

Part Three: What's Your Market?

Analyzing your market is the part of the business plan that takes the most homework. If you're in business, you've already done some of your research by developing clients and bumping heads with your competitors.

Your market analysis should include:

- *Descriptions of how you expect design services and the particular types of clients you serve to grow in the coming years.* Is your market subject to economic ups and downs, and where is it now? Is it seasonal? And what are the future prospects for your services?
- *A listing and description of your competitors, how many there are, their strengths and weaknesses.*
- *A profile of your likely clients, including their number, demographics and other key traits.*
- *A description of where you fit in the industry.* What's your competitive edge? How does your service meet a need that isn't provided by anyone else, or how do you meet those needs better? How do you compare to competitors in terms of price, quality, scope of service or specialized know-how?

Part Four: What's Your Strategy?

Defining your strategy flows naturally from what you've already done with your plan. The elements of your strategic planning include:

- *Marketing, promotion and sales strategy*: How are you going to reach the potential clients you've identified in your market analysis?
- *Revenue projections*: Based on the history of your business or your preliminary contacts with potential clients, how much do you expect to be able to bill for your first year? The following years? Do a month-by-month projection for the first year, based in part on any seasonal patterns you found earlier.
- *Pricing*: How much do you plan to charge? For an in-depth discussion of pricing, see pages 85-90.
- *Growth projections*: Do you plan to expand,

Business Plan Checklist

Your business plan should include the following things:

- Company analysis
- Service analysis, including:
  - Which services you provide
  - Why they're better than the competition
  - How you provide them
  - Where you're located
  - How you'll expand service in the future
- Market analysis, including:
  - Which market you're targeting
  - Profile of your clients
  - Is the market growing?
  - Description of your competition
  - Where you fit in the market
- Strategic plan
  - Marketing/promotion/sales strategy
  - Revenue projections
  - Pricing policy
  - Growth projections
- Financial plan
  - Balance sheet
  - Profit-and-loss statement
  - Profit-and-loss projection
  - Cash flow projection
  - Source of funds or debt schedule

You can get help with your plan through:

- U.S. Small Business Administration Publications
- Advice from the Service Corps for Retired Executives
- Library research
- Specialized business plan software

or do you only want to make the most money you can with the resources you have now? If you plan to expand, will you hire employees, add partners, or hire contractors when your work load outgrows current capacity? Will you outgrow your current quarters? Will you need to invest in more computer equipment? What's your expansion timetable?

Getting Focused

When Debbie Dent left her job with a Cincinnati service bureau to start her own business, she didn't have a business plan. She had something better: an agreement to design and produce mechanicals for a large project that would pay for a computer to start her business. She also had enough money in the bank to buy her computer system before she got paid for the job.

That got Epic Design off to a fast start. At first, Debbie didn't miss having a business plan. After all, she had raised what capital she needed from savings. She worked out of her home, so overhead was low. Her first job got her past the break-even point. And so much work came in from referrals that she didn't have to worry about marketing.

"If I hadn't had my husband's outside income to rely on, it might not have been such a good idea to not have a business plan," Debbie admits. In her second year, she started seeing more need for a plan. "As time went on, I was spinning my wheels a lot and putting out fires as they came up," she says. "The business really had no direction."

The first year brought steady work. But the second year was more like a roller-coaster ride of frantic activity followed by slow periods. Epic Design was still successful, but it was getting out of control.

This table of contents from the business plan for Willow Design shows the detailed steps the Dents went through in outlining their business strategy.

Section I: Description of Willow Design
   A. Overview of Willow Design
   B. Business Philosophy
   C. Business Goals
   D. Location
   E. Typical Job Flow
Section II: Marketing Plan
   A. Overview of the Market
   B. Current Client List of Market
   C. Potential Customers
   D. Promotion Strategy
   E. Competition
Section III: Organization
   A. Management
   B. Sub-contractors
   C. Legal Sructure
   D. Bookkeeping and Record Keeping
   E. Licenses and Permits
   F. Resources
Section IV: Financial Data
   A. Initial Investment
   B. Insurance Coverage
   C. Balance Sheet
   D. Profit and Loss Statement
   E. Breakeven Analyses
   F. Personal Credit Report
   G. Personal Federal Income Tax Returns
Section V: Financial Projections
   A. 1990 Pro Forma Income Statement
   B. 1991 Pro Forma Income Statement
   C. 1992 Pro Forma Income Statement
Appendices
   Appendix A: Sales Brochure (Portfolio review available)
   Appendix B: Equipment List
   Appendix C: Resumes of R. Wade and Deborah K. Dent

At the same time, Debbie's husband, Wade, was considering quitting his job as a chemical engineer to join her in the business and take over administration of it. For Wade to leave behind a good income as an engineer, however, the couple felt they had to have a clear direction for the business. And the only way to do that was with a business plan.

"Doing a business plan stinks," Debbie says. "It takes a lot of time, and it's low on your priority list, because other things pay. But once it's done, it's very easy to revise, and it really helps you stay focused." To make time for the plan, the Dents went away for a weekend with a portable computer and their spreadsheet and word processing software. "That was the only way we could get it done," Debbie says, "by leaving our home environment and focusing on one task for the entire weekend."

The hard work paid off, Wade says. "The business plan really helps you see some inconsistencies between what you think you're trying to offer your clients vs. what you really have to offer," he says. "You have to analyze the market, your competition, your own strengths and abilities to provide services to the market."

What they came out with was really two businesses. Epic Design would continue to provide electronic design and publishing services to a broad range of clients. A new company, Willow Design, would combine Wade's experience with computers and Debbie's experience with design by providing consultation to designers who were setting up their own desktop computer systems.

"We didn't realize until we did the business plan that to survive, we were going to have to specialize by providing services to the design community—ad agencies, graphic designers, print houses and typographers," Wade says. It didn't make sense for Willow Design to target all kinds of clients when much bigger computer training and consulting companies in town already were established in the market. But Willow Design's specialized knowledge of computer applications for designers and its low overhead made it perfect for competing against the big companies in its own niche.

The plan also helped the Dents analyze their expenses and cash flow and project their needs for investment in new equipment for both businesses over time. "A business plan really helps you focus on what's important," Wade says.

Just to make sure their focus was good, the Dents showed their business plan to three banks, even though they didn't need to borrow money. They figured it's the job of bank officers to evaluate business plans. So there was no better place to get a qualified, objective appraisal. "Everyone we showed it to thought the plan was well thought through and concise, and they said they would loan us money," Debbie says. The Dents still didn't borrow. But the exercise gave them the confidence they needed for Wade to quit his job and successfully expand the business.

Part Five: Will You Make Money? (Financial Analysis)

All your work boils down to this bottom line. Analyzing your current and future financial situation—income, profit, costs, etc.—is the most complicated section of the business plan and may require help from an accountant or other business adviser. But if your business is small and uncomplicated, you may be able to get through this yourself.

Elements of the financial analysis part of your business plan include:

■ *Balance sheet*: This shows the financial condition of your business at a given time. The balance sheet shows assets (such as your computer equipment, money in your business bank accounts or anything of value your business owns), liabilities (anything your business owes anyone else) and equity or book value (what's left over after you subtract liabilities from assets). This may be an actual balance sheet or a "pro forma" version, which is a projection for your new business.

■ *Profit-and-loss statement*: This is a calculation of your revenue, expenses and net profit or loss for the past year. If you're just starting your business, you won't have an income statement to report.

■ *Profit-and-loss projection*: Just like a profit-and-loss statement, only it projects what will happen over the coming months and years rather than what's already happened. This projection becomes your budget.

■ *Projected cash flow*: This projects when your business will spend cash and when it will get cash from clients. It's a valuable tool to forecast how much credit or cash reserve you'll need.

■ *Source of funds or debt schedules*: For a start-up business, this may show the sources of funds, such as bank loans, personal savings or capital paid in by partners. It also will show how you plan to use the start-up funds—for example, buying computer equipment, fixing up an office or setting aside a cash reserve to cover lean times. For an existing business, this schedule shows how much is owed to whom and when payment is due.

Preparing Your Plan

If you've answered the questions above, you're likely done with your business plan. But if you intend to show your plan to bankers or anyone else for business purposes, add some bells and whistles.

At the beginning of the plan, write an executive summary that previews each section. This need be no more than a paragraph for each section, but should be enough to get the point across. Summarize your plan at the end with a hard-hitting message about why your business will work.

The graphic presentation of your business plan is very important. Because you're a designer, the medium is the message. Your plan is an example of what you can do for clients, and the loan officer may ask consciously or subconsciously if he or she would want to pay for such work. Pay attention to the typography and the paper. You can turn your plan into a brochure that shows examples of your work and presents financial information in graphics and text. Perhaps you can work elements of existing promotional pieces into the plan. But don't get carried away. Presenting your business plan too extravagantly could make the bank question how wisely you spend money.

Resources for Help

A business plan may seem terribly complex, but there's plenty of help available. The two best alternatives are publications by the U.S. Small Business Administration (S.B.A.) and software packages that provide templates to guide you.

S.B.A. publications are a good alternative for two reasons: they're cheap, and they're easy to use. If you belong to a local chamber of commerce, you may even get them free. Otherwise, they cost $1 or $2. Information from the S.B.A. is available by calling (800) 368-5855.

An S.B.A. booklet titled "The Business Plan for Home-based Business" is great even if you don't have a home office. It provides straightforward sections on decisions to make before you go into business. And it has good sections on preparing the financial aspects of a business plan. Another S.B.A. booklet, "Business Plan for Small Service Firms," contains useful worksheets for cash flow and income projections.

If publications aren't enough to get you through the plan, another S.B.A. service may help. The Service Corps of Retired Executives (SCORE) is a branch of the S.B.A. that provides all aspects of free business advice from retired executives to small businesses. Your local chamber of commerce may put you in touch with a local SCORE volunteer, or contact SCORE at 409 Third Street, NW, Washington, D.C. 20416, (202) 653-6279.

Professional help from an accountant or management consultant also may also be in order. The problem is expense. Expect to pay an hourly rate at least as high as your own fee, and probably higher. Plus, you'll invest some of your own precious time. If you choose a professional, it should be an individual or small firm that can relate to the needs of a small business. Ideally, it should be a client with whom you could barter, or at least use the experience to help cement a business relationship.

Another option is putting your computer to work in preparing your plan. Several business plan software packages are on the market, but some are only for IBM or compatible computers. The PC-only versions tend to package the program with spreadsheet and word processing programs you may not need. And they're expensive—in the $300 to $500 range. Business Plan Toolkit and BizPlanBuilder are better buys in the $100 range. They run on Macs or PCs and work with the word processing and spreadsheet software you already have. Even at this low price, the software represents an expense that may be unnecessary. If you can figure out the software, you can probably figure out how to do the plan without it.

You may need to do library research for the market analysis section of your plan. The annual U.S. Industrial Outlook published by the U.S. Department of Commerce is a good place to start for national statistics on the kind of companies you hope to have as clients. Articles in business publications also can spell out trends that will affect your market. Libraries in major metropolitan areas will have such articles indexed by industry and other subject headings, stored on CD-ROM drives and accessible by computer terminals.

How Much Should I Charge?

Deciding how much to charge clients is one of the most important parts of planning a business. Not only does your hourly rate determine your income, it also may decide whether you get a job. It even plays a role in establishing your image in the marketplace. Pricing is also one of the hardest business decisions you'll make. There's no magic formula, guidebook or method that works in every situation.

Except for those rare times when a client tells you the budget and states the terms up front, the responsibility for setting rates is yours. You may set rates on a per-project basis. That's great for your client, who won't have any surprises when the bill comes. But it makes your life a lot more unpredictable. The same type of job can take vastly different amounts of time, depending on how clearly the client communicates what she or he wants and how many revisions she or he demands before the job is done.

An hourly rate is the only way to have any idea if a project will be worth your while. And even if you quote estimates for projects, as most professional graphic artists do, you should base that fee on an hourly rate that takes your overhead and income needs into account. Your estimate should clearly state the work you will perform for that amount and what happens if the project goes over your budgeted time. Some designers don't charge extra if a project runs over because of their own efforts. But if a project runs over because of changes the customer makes after the job starts, you should charge extra. Experienced designers may be able to estimate such "grief and aggravation" charges before the job starts. Until you reach that point, you'll take a bath if you don't specify extra charges for midcourse corrections.

You can arrive at your business' hourly rate two ways. One is theoretical—calculating your monthly overhead plus the profit for your business or the personal income you hope to make. The other is the more practical market-driven method, which involves finding out what your competition is charging and basing your rates on that. Both methods are important. The first ensures you'll make money for your work. The second ensures you'll get work.

The Hourly Rate Formula

The hourly rate formula is a fairly easy way to figure out how much you or your company must charge to meet an income or profit goal. It calculates hourly overhead, which is what you must spend each month whether you work or not. And it adds an hourly breakdown of what you hope to make. Here's a line-by-line explanation:

1. *Fixed overhead: These are monthly expenses that are usually the same over the course of a year.*

Office rent/mortgage: If you run your business from leased office space, this is pretty straightforward. If you have a home office, it's more of a judgment call. You may want to include the percentage of rent or mortgage that corresponds to the percentage of your home's size the office occupies. You may not have gotten a bigger house or apartment just so you could have extra space for your business, so in a sense, this isn't a business expense. But it's certainly a legitimate item to include in overhead, since you may include it as an expense for taxes. (Note: Include depreciation of the value of your home in this calculation. The simplest way is to divide the fair market value of your home by 31.5, which is the number of years of useful life the Internal Revenue Service assigns to business real property. Then, take the business percentage of your home as depreciation.)

Equipment rent and depreciation: This is for your computer equipment or other business property. If you lease your equipment, just include the lease payments. If you own it, include the depreciation. The estimated useful life for computer equipment is six years, according to the Internal Revenue Service. So divide by six the purchase price or the fair market value of the equipment at the time you started using it. Even if you use accelerated depreciation methods for taxes, which will be discussed later (see pages 92-93), use the ordinary method to calculate overhead. For office furniture, the useful life is ten years.

Interest: This is for nonmortgage interest on your computer equipment or business property.

Health insurance: This is for premiums for

Setting Rates at the Outset

Like many beginning desktop designers and publishers, Sharon Baldwin Sittner of Cincinnati didn't want to price herself out of the market when she started business in 1987. Because she was new to the work—and the technology—she was reluctant to price her services too high.

Sittner's first job was editing and creating mechanicals for a construction company's in-house newsletter, a job she got through a friend. "When I started doing the newsletter, I had no experience at this kind of thing whatsoever," she admits. "I was still going to college part time and didn't have a degree yet."

With those factors in mind, she decided to bill her time at the bargain rate of $10 an hour. She estimated the four-page newsletter would take ten hours of work, including typing, editing, making calls to fill in gaps in the information submitted to her, taking mechanicals

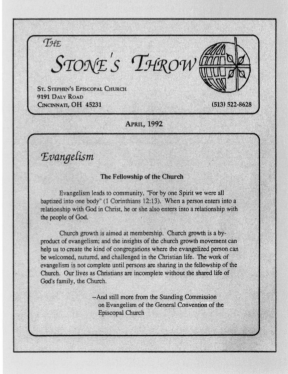

to the printer and delivering printed copies. So she gave an estimate of $100 per issue.

Sittner says she underestimated the amount of travel and organizational time the job involved, especially in dealing with the printer. By the time she had done the newsletter for two years, Sittner had almost doubled the per-issue charge to $190. And over four years she's doubled her hourly rate.

Compared to other desktop publishers who do similar work, her rate is on the low end but is competitive, she says—although she's considering raising it. "I think it's probably still too low," she says, laughing. "Nobody's ever complained about it."

One factor that lets her stay competitive is low overhead. She has a relatively low-cost IBM-compatible computer and laser printer. Most of her competitors use higher-cost Macs. And her office takes up only a corner of her kitchen.

A mother of three, Sittner only wants part-time work and a little extra income along with the flexibility to care for her children after school and in the summer. Her desktop publishing business provides all those things.

One complicating factor in setting rates, she says, is that her services span different fields with different rate structures. She considered herself primarily a freelance writer and editor when she went into business. Though most of her work involves desktop publishing, much of it also includes writing and editing.

Out-of-pocket expenses like printing are paid by clients and billed directly, so Sittner doesn't have the cash flow worries of a printer's bill but doesn't get the customary markup, either.

She lost her first client when her husband was promoted to a job with a competitive company and her work on the newsletter was considered a conflict of interest. Even though the fee for that work was low, the experience was valuable: That job still pays off in terms of client referrals, she says. She hopes to land a job doing an association newsletter in the future as a result of her experience, since the manager of that former client also heads a local business group.

Sharon Baldwin Sittner produces newsletters for a variety of clients, including a local church.

Community News

Come Run - Come Walk...

Working in Neighborhoods, Inc. is sponsoring its ninth annual "Be A W.I.N.ner At Heart" 5K Run/Fitness Walk. The race will be held Saturday, April 4, at 9:00 a.m. at the Boat Harbor at Winton Woods. The Entry fee is $6; family rate $8. Souvenir T-Shirts available for $8. For further information, call the W.I.N. office at 541-4109, Kathy Cucchetti at 522-8986, or Mary Jackson at 541-8126.

And Speaking of Winton Woods...

The fifth annual Winton Woods Cleanup is scheduled (rain or shine) for Saturday, April 25, from 8:45 a.m. to 12:00 noon. Last year, over 300 volunteers and 100 members of the National Guard collected over 6 tons of trash and debris! Meet at Kestrel Point. A free picnic lunch will follow for all volunteers. See you there!

Spring Boutique Sale at Providence...

The Providence Hospital Auxiliary Crafters and Designers are having a Spring Boutique Sale April 1-3 in the hospital's visitor's lobby. Beautiful silk floral arrangements and handcrafted items will be available. All proceeds will benefit the hospital. The sale will be held from 3-7 p.m. on April 1; 7:30 a.m.-8 p.m. on April 2; and 8:30 a.m.-1:00 p.m. on April 3.

All Saints Episcopal Church Concert...

The All Saints Church choir will be singing at a Washington Cathedral worship service on May 3, 1992. Come and get a sneak preview at their pre-Washington Cathedral concert at All Saints, Pleasant Ridge, on Sunday, April 5, at 4:00 p.m. There will be a tea following the concert.

BIRTHDAYS

April 1	Bea Therrien
April 5	Pam Bodenstein
April 7	Pat Jones
April 8	Chuck Healy
April 8	Marie Waag
April 10	Billie Peeno
April 11	Shirley Dillon
April 17	Cheryl McBee
April 29	Josh Windsor

ANNIVERSARIES

April 10	Bob & Lola Cooper
April 13	Barton & Pat Jones
April 15	Bill & Dorothy Boyd
April 26	Bill & Taffy Billman

Money Is Always an Object

When clients say money is no object, Rebecca Lodge doesn't believe them. The owner and sole employee of Cincinnati's Lodge & Associates has had clients who want to project that image — but when the bill comes, they care.

"Even if money is no object for them, it's still an object for me," Lodge says. "I never want to put myself in a position of having to defend my bill." So when clients don't ask for an estimate, Lodge gives them one anyway. "I want clients to have the same expectations about a job that I do," she says. "I may be thinking $500 and they may be thinking $50, but I won't know that unless we talk about it first."

Lodge's background in sales for an engineering consultant and her husband's background in cost accounting for construction projects have made her very sensitive to clients' budget needs. She strives to be very accurate in estimating jobs and letting clients know exactly what they'll get for that money. "If their budget expectation is unrealistic, I just tell them that flat out," she says. Then she presents a range of options at a range of prices.

Lodge cites the example of a woman who left a national employment agency to start her own. She wanted postcard-size mailers with four-color photographs, similar to the ones that cost her old company 3¢ apiece to produce. But her old company used hundreds of thousands, and she was considering a press run of less than a thousand. The photography alone might cost her $10,000, Lodge says. "If we had just proceeded without talking about the cost, it would have been a real disaster."

Lodge's estimates are based on several years of experience and two filing cabinets full of detailed information on past jobs. When she needs to make a bid, she compares it in her mind to past jobs and pulls the file on that job. She's careful to track how much time was for her own mistakes, which she knows she won't repeat and thus doesn't add to the estimate. Estimating was harder for her first jobs, Lodge says. But she knew how many words a minute she could type and guessed on the rest.

Lodge makes it a policy not to go over budget. She doesn't charge to fix her own mistakes. But when clients want to make revisions or change the scope of a project, she makes sure they know exactly how much their revisions will change the cost and deadline for the project.

Lodge never charges a generic piece rate or a per-page rate, because every job is different. "It takes a lot more time to squeeze four typewritten pages of copy into a postcard than a couple of paragraphs," she says. So her estimates and her bills are always based on an hourly rate.

At first, Lodge based her hourly rate on how much she needed to make in the first year to pay back her investment. She was willing to work cheap the first year to get established and build a clientele. Since she set up a home office, that investment included her computer system, office furniture and supplies. "Everybody told me I couldn't do it, but I did," she says. "I didn't pay myself anything and I worked long hours, but I did it."

After paying off her initial investment and increasing her work load, she also had more work than she could handle herself. She hired typists and proofreaders as independent contractors to avoid payroll taxes and keep overhead low. She

your company group health insurance plan. But even if you pay your own health insurance, it's fair to include this as an overhead expense for anyone who's self-employed. After all, it's figured into the overhead cost of almost any company with employees.

Other business insurance: Nonhealth insurance for business property, casualty, liability, etc.

2. *Averaged expenses: These are overhead expenses that need to be estimated for the year, since they're more subject to change than the fixed expenses.*

Employee wages: This is only if you have any regular employees. Don't include your own salary in this, even if your business pays you a salary. Your share is taken into consideration later in the formula. The cost of independent con-

started factoring their fees into the estimates plus a 15 percent markup.

She also has raised her rates from year to year, based on information she acquired about what clients pay elsewhere and what other businesses charge.

"I've seen people lower their rates the hungrier they get," she says. "But there's an attitude among clients that they're not going to get much if they're not paying much. People go out of business for that reason."

Lodge once lost an account to a secretarial service that offered desktop publishing at rock-bottom rates. The service even had overhead Lodge didn't, with a commercial office and monthly rent. "I told the client I couldn't afford to work for that rate, but if they could get the same thing for less, go for it," Lodge says. She also told them they were welcome back anytime. Six months later, the service folded and Lodge had her client back.

She cautions new desktop designers and publishers against ignoring overhead and future investment needs when calculating their hourly rates. "Don't think just because you charge $25 an hour that that's what you make," Lodge says. "Have you put anything in there for your costs and for profit?" Profit isn't just what you keep, she cautions. Some of it must be put away for investing in new software and equipment to keep pace with rapidly changing technology.

tractors or temporary employees added for specific jobs should be billed to the clients.

Other averaged expenses: These include costs such as utilities, laser paper and other costs that may vary month to month. If you're starting out, you'll have to make your best guess about what your annual costs for such things are, and divide them by twelve. If you've been in business one year, you've got hard data to use. Don't forget to adjust figures for inflation, using the Consumer Price Index or information about price increases from suppliers.

3. *Total overhead: Add fixed overhead and averaged expenses to get your total overhead.*

4. *Billable hours: Divide your total overhead by your estimated annual billable hours to come up with the overhead component of your hourly rate.* Don't confuse billable hours with total working hours. For a one- or two-person operation, count on spending at least 25 percent of your working hours on administration and marketing. Even if you have employees, you can't expect more than six hours a day of their time to be billable when you take staff meetings, training and other nonclient time into account.

5. *Income or profit goal: This is a personal measure of what you hope to make per hour for your efforts, plus additional earnings you hope to retain for future investment in the company (new computer equipment, etc.).* For a one-person operation, you may want to base this annual figure in part on what you used to make at an earlier job. It should correspond to your level of experience, too. If you've been a designer for five years, your work is worth more than if you've been doing it only one year. Your cost of living is another factor to consider.

6. *Divide the income/profit goal by the same billable hours figure arrived at earlier.*

7. *Hourly rate: The hourly rate you arrive at gives you an idea of what you must make to meet your income goal.*

Other costs you incur, such as for service bureaus, courier services and printing, usually are billed separately from your hourly rate. Most design studios, ad agencies and desktop designers and publishers mark up the cost of these services by 15 percent to 20 percent, and some even more. That compensates them for the risk they take in paying vendors' bills before their clients pay them. Some clients may prefer to be billed directly to avoid the markup. If you choose to absorb the cost of any of these services, figure them into your overhead.

The figure you come up with is not necessarily what you'll end up charging. You can't set prices in a vacuum. Ultimately, what the market is willing to pay will determine what you can

Hourly Rate Formula

This chart shows the different types of costs and profit considerations that go into setting an hourly rate.

Overhead expenses:	
Fixed overhead:	**$00,000**
Office rent/mortgage:	000
Equipment rent/depreciation:	000
Interest:	000
Health insurance:	000
Other business insurance:	000
Other:	000
Averaged expenses:	**$00,000**
Employee wages:	000
Advertising:	000
Utilities:	000
Office and business supplies:	000
Bookkeeping/accounting:	000
Taxes (Business taxes other than income taxes) and licenses:	000
Legal expense:	000
Vehicle expense:	000
Travel/entertainment expense:	000
Maintenance:	000
Publications:	000
Other:	000
Total overhead:	**$00,000**
Add fixed overhead and averaged expenses.	
Total operating costs per hour:	**$000**
Divide total overhead by billable hours per year.	
Total income goal per hour:	**$000**
Divide profit goal by billable hours per year.	
Hourly rate:	**$000**
Add total operating costs per hour and total income goal per hour.	

charge. But the figure is important for giving you an idea of what's fair and what you must make to meet your goals.

If the rate you arrive at is more than the market will bear, you must make adjustments. Those include cutting overhead, lowering your income expectations, or finding ways to boost productivity or your billable hours to bring your hourly rates into line. If your rate turns out to be less than market rates, you're in luck. You can raise your hourly fee to the going rate or leave it low to undercut competitors. A compromise between your rate and the prevailing rate may be the best strategy, since you'll make more

than you expected and still keep a competitive edge.

Productivity is a wild card that can make a big difference in what you can charge. If you can turn out twice the work in an hour as someone less proficient, then an hour of your work is twice as valuable. The longer you're in business, the better you'll get. And the better you get, the easier it is to justify higher hourly rates.

The tremendous productivity increases generated by designing and publishing with a desktop computer have changed the way some designers charge. They may have higher rates for time spent on the computer than for more con-

Bartering With Other Businesses

Bartering is a great way to buy equipment or services for your business without tapping cash. Potential vendors who are also potential customers—printers, copywriters, computer stores—are also potential barter partners.

When Icon Graphics Inc., decided to add a new MacIntosh SE 30 to its Rochester, New York, business, the company found a computer store that also needed design work. "We knew how much we could get the computer for with cash," says Icon partner Steve BonDurant. "So we told the client what we wanted to spend, and that was enough to give him some profit. We discounted that on his bill." Icon ended up using the SE 30 on the computer store's job. "That made a nice down payment, and we billed the balance later when the work was done," BonDurant says. "Most times, we don't get a deposit, so that really was a good deal."

If you can't find others interested in bartering, a local barter club may be the answer. The clubs usually work on credit points: You accumulate credits by doing work for other businesses in the club, and you spend them when you buy the other members' services or products. The barter club makes money either from your membership fees or a percentage of transactions, or both.

Improving cash flow is the best reason to barter, since it saves your spending cash to pay for things you need. But for service businesses, bartering may not be a very good deal in tax terms. The Internal Revenue Service expects you to report the fair market value of anything you receive in barter as income. But you can't deduct the value of the service you provide. That means you pay more taxes than you might have if everything had been on a cash basis. For instance, if you did $1,000 worth of work for cash and then bought a laser printer with the money, you could deduct that $1,000 worth of equipment from your $1,000 in income. If you trade $1,000 worth of work for the laser printer, you have to report the $1,000 value of the printer as income—but you can't deduct the value of the work you did. So you end up paying tax on $1,000 more than if you'd worked on a cash basis.

You may be able to get around this problem by setting up your barter arrangement as a cash transaction on paper. For instance, you could get a $1,000 check from the computer store and immediately buy the computer with it. There's nothing wrong with that. What the Internal Revenue Service is on watch for is people who accept bartered goods and services without reporting them.

---

ventional types of work. That's because the computer has made them more productive and, therefore, made computer time worth more. Some designers charge separate rates for conceptual time, meeting time, travel time and other categories, too. Conceptual and meeting time usually commands top dollar, because it involves some of the most highly skilled work.

Researching Market Rates
Before you set your rates, you have to know what others like you charge. It's not that hard. Here are three ways to do it:

■ *The direct approach*: Get to know desktop designers and publishers—or people who use those services—and find out what the going rates are. If you're leaving a job at a design stu-

dio, ad agency or related concern, you may have a good idea of what the market rates are from your experience there.

■ *The directory approach*: National organizations, such as the Graphic Artists Guild and the American Institute of Graphic Arts, have published pricing guides. They can serve as a guide for you on both hourly rates and overall bids for jobs. Designers outside large metropolitan markets, however, report that the rates tend to be on the high side. See if your local desktop design and publishing group has done rate studies. If not, persuade it to do one.

■ *The sneaky approach*: Call, or get a friend to call, your competitors to get their bids on work. This is probably the most scientific way to test the waters in your area and give you a good range of the highs and lows. Unfortu-

IRS Schedule C provides the basic categories of income and expenses you'll compile as an independent business. You'll probably be using the cash-accounting method (Line F), since it's the simplest way to keep books.

Not all items may apply to you. For example, unless you get into the printing or publishing end of the business, inventory considerations won't apply to you.

Most expenses are fairly easy to categorize. But some things, like the costs of independent contractors, need to go under miscellaneous expenses. Try to break down miscellaneous expenses as completely as possible on the lines provided. Large, unexplained, miscellaneous expenses are more likely to draw scrutiny from the IRS.

nately, it's also sneaky. If others in your field find out you've been spying on them, they may resent it. And that could cut you out of valuable networking opportunities.

Your research likely will yield a range of rates, which will depend on the experience and skill of the person or company doing the work. Once you've identified the range, compare yourself with others in the market to get an idea of where you fit.

One of the big advantages of desktop design and publishing is that it takes less time than traditional methods and is therefore cheaper. So competitive pricing always will be an important part of this business. But pricing your services too low can dig you into a rut of low-paying customers interested solely in price, not quality.

It's tempting for a new business to get work quickly by low-ball pricing—pricing at or below the low end of rates charged by similarly skilled designers. You may succeed in getting work this way, but there are pitfalls. First, it can damage your reputation. Few people expect great work from an underpriced bidder. You could lose out on some great jobs because your price is too low. Also, even if you land a job with a low-ball price, you may make little money on it. And once you've established a rate with clients, it can be hard to raise prices on future projects. So if you're thinking of a low-ball price as a way to get your foot in the door, consider what life will be like once you get in the foyer.

Once you arrive at an hourly rate, it still will need to be flexible. You won't quote the same rate to the corner store that you would to a Fortune 500 company. The Fortune 500 company probably will be comfortable with prevailing rates you'd find in pricing guides of national organizations. A small local business or a nonprofit group might not.

Tax Planning

Once your business is profitable—or even if it isn't at first—tax planning will help you make the most of your money. The basis of your business, your computer system, is one of the most important aspects of your tax planning.

You can deduct from your taxable income any legitimate expense your business incurs, provided you have a receipt or other documentation. The Internal Revenue Service applies the "ordinary" and "necessary" rules in judging the validity of a business expense. That means the expenses should be ordinary for your profession and necessary for carrying out your business.

Computers, Peripherals and Other Equipment
Deducting the cost of your computer system may involve some fairly extensive paperwork, depending on where your business is. If your computer is used in a regular business office, there's no question that it's a legitimate business deduction. If you work from your home, it can be more complicated. Computers and peripheral equipment are classified as "listed" property by the Internal Revenue Service, which means they commonly have both business and personal uses. (Cellular telephones, automobiles and entertainment equipment also fall under this heading.) If your home office clearly fits the definition of a qualified home office, your computer equipment won't fall under the listed property category—so it's an unquestioned business expense. If your work space doesn't qualify as a deductible home office, then you can only deduct the percentage of your computer that corresponds to what proportion it's used for business.

Even if your computer is in what seems to be a legitimate home office, it might be a good idea to document your computer use in case the Internal Revenue Service denies your home-office deduction in an audit someday. The airtight way to document the percentage your computer is used for business is to keep a log. Record the date and hours each time you use your computer and whether that use is personal or business. For business use, briefly describe the business purpose. If less than 50 percent of the computer time you log is for business, you must depreciate the business percentage of the system's cost in equal installments over six years. Depreciation refers to the amount of your equipment expense you can write off over time. Most business expenses are fully deductible the first year. But equipment with a useful life of more than a year generally must be depreciated over several years.

If you use the computer more than 50 percent for business, you can use an accelerated depreciation method, which allows you to deduct the business percentage of its cost over five years and up to 35 percent the first year. You

may even be allowed to write off the entire cost the year you buy the computer system under Section 179 of the tax code.

Desks, tables, chairs, bookshelves, filing cabinets and other office furnishings are also deductible expenses if you use them in your business. Like computers and other equipment with useful lives of more than a year, office equipment is subject to depreciation rules. You may depreciate it over seven years or, under Section 179, deduct the full amount the year you buy it.

Usually, business equipment and property must be depreciated over several years. But you may be able to take advantage of Section 179, which allows up to $10,000 of business equipment to be fully deducted the year it's purchased. Computer equipment, cars and cellular phones used less than 50 percent for business can't be deducted. But if business use is 100 percent, you can deduct those items fully. And if the use is between 50 and 100 percent, you can deduct that percentage of the expense. Section 179 and other depreciation costs can't be used to deduct more than you make from your business. But you can carry over Section 179 expenses to future years if you don't have income to deduct them against now.

Some of the equipment you use in your business you may have already owned as personal property. You can still deduct such equipment as business expenses. To deduct items converted from personal to business use, first determine the fair market value at the time of the conversion. That value can be depreciated over several years, according to the depreciation rules for the item.

I.R.S. Publication 534 provides more details on depreciation and Section 179, including a full set of depreciation tables for various classes of property.

Home-Office Expenses
If you run your business from a traditional office, the rent or other costs are fully deductible. One advantage of having a home office is that part of your home may also become deductible as a business asset.

Desktop design and publishing lends itself well to home offices. But the home-office deduction is difficult to qualify for. And many

Form **4562**

Department of the Treasury
Internal Revenue Service (M)

Name(s) shown on return

Depreciation and Amortization
(Including Information on Listed Property)

▶ See separate instructions. ▶ Attach this form to your return.

OMB No. 1545-0172

19**91**

Attachment Sequence No. **67**

Identifying number

Business or activity to which this form relates

Part I Election To Expense Certain Tangible Property (Section 179) (Note: If you have any "Listed Property," complete Part V)

1 Maximum dollar limitation (see instructions)	1	$10,000
2 Total cost of section 179 property placed in service during the tax year (see instructions)	2	
3 Threshold cost of section 179 property before reduction in limitation	3	$200,000
4 Reduction in limitation—Subtract line 3 from line 2, but do not enter less than -0-	4	
5 Dollar limitation for tax year—Subtract line 4 from line 1, but do not enter less than -0-	5	

6

(a) Description of property	(b) Cost	(c) Elected cost

7 Listed property—Enter amount from line 26	7	
8 Total elected cost of section 179 property—Add amounts in column (c), lines 6 and 7	8	
9 Tentative deduction—Enter the lesser of line 5 or line 8	9	
10 Carryover of disallowed deduction from 1990 (see instructions)	10	
11 Taxable income limitation—Enter the lesser of taxable income or line 5 (see instructions)	11	
12 Section 179 expense deduction—Add lines 9 and 10, but do not enter more than line 11	12	
13 Carryover of disallowed deduction to 1992—Add lines 9 and 10, less line 12 ▶ 13		

Note: Do not use Part II or Part III below for automobiles, certain other vehicles, cellular telephones, computers, or property used for entertainment, recreation, or amusement (listed property). Instead, use Part V for listed property.

Part II MACRS Depreciation For Assets Placed in Service ONLY During Your 1991 Tax Year (Do Not Include Listed Property)

(a) Classification of property	(b) Mo. and yr. placed in service	(c) Basis for depreciation (Business/investment use only—see instructions)	(d) Recovery period	(e) Convention	(f) Method	(g) Depreciation deduction
14 General Depreciation System (GDS) (see instructions):						
a 3-year property						
b 5-year property						
c 7-year property						
d 10-year property						
e 15-year property						
f 20-year property						
g Residential rental property			27.5 yrs.	MM	S/L	
			27.5 yrs.	MM	S/L	
h Nonresidential real property			31.5 yrs.	MM	S/L	
			31.5 yrs.	MM	S/L	
15 Alternative Depreciation System (ADS) (see instructions):						
a Class life					S/L	
b 12-year			12 yrs.		S/L	
c 40-year			40 yrs.	MM	S/L	

Part III Other Depreciation (Do Not Include Listed Property)

16 GDS and ADS deductions for assets placed in service in tax years beginning before 1991 (see instructions)	16	
17 Property subject to section 168(f)(1) election (see instructions)	17	
18 ACRS and other depreciation (see instructions)	18	

Part IV Summary

19 Listed property—Enter amount from line 25	19	
20 Total—Add deductions on line 12, lines 14 and 15 in column (g), and lines 16 through 19. Enter here and on the appropriate lines of your return. (Partnerships and S corporations—see instructions)	20	
21 For assets shown above and placed in service during the current year, enter the portion of the basis attributable to section 263A costs (see instructions)	21	

For Paperwork Reduction Act Notice, see page 1 of the separate instructions.   Cat. No. 12906N   Form **4562** (1991)

155

Form 4562 (1991)   Page **2**

Part V Listed Property.—Automobiles, Certain Other Vehicles, Cellular Telephones, Computers, and Property Used for Entertainment, Recreation, or Amusement

If you are using the standard mileage rate or deducting vehicle lease expense, complete columns (a) through (c) of Section A, all of Section B, and Section C if applicable.

Section A.—Depreciation (Caution: See instructions for limitations for automobiles.)

22a Do you have evidence to support the business/investment use claimed? ☐ Yes ☐ No   22b If "Yes," is the evidence written? ☐ Yes ☐ No

(a) Type of property (list vehicles first)	(b) Date placed in service	(c) Business/investment use percentage	(d) Cost or other basis	(e) Basis for depreciation (Business/investment use only)	(f) Recovery period	(g) Method/Convention	(h) Depreciation deduction	(i) Elected section 179 cost
23 Property used more than 50% in a qualified business use (see instructions):								
		%						
		%						
		%						
24 Property used 50% or less in a qualified business use (see instructions):								
		%				S/L –		
		%				S/L –		
		%				S/L –		
25 Add amounts in column (h). Enter the total here and on line 19, page 1					25			
26 Add amounts in column (i). Enter the total here and on line 7, page 1						26		

Section B.—Information Regarding Use of Vehicles—If you deduct expenses for vehicles:
• Always complete this section for vehicles used by a sole proprietor, partner, or other "more than 5% owner," or related person.
• If you provided vehicles to your employees, first answer the questions in Section C to see if you meet an exception to completing this section for those vehicles.

	(a) Vehicle 1	(b) Vehicle 2	(c) Vehicle 3	(d) Vehicle 4	(e) Vehicle 5	(f) Vehicle 6
27 Total business/investment miles driven during the year (DO NOT include commuting miles)						
28 Total commuting miles driven during the year						
29 Total other personal (noncommuting) miles driven						
30 Total miles driven during the year—Add lines 27 through 29						

	Yes	No	Yes	No	Yes	No	Yes	No	Yes	No	Yes	No
31 Was the vehicle available for personal use during off-duty hours?												
32 Was the vehicle used primarily by a more than 5% owner or related person?												
33 Is another vehicle available for personal use?												

Section C.—Questions for Employers Who Provide Vehicles for Use by Their Employees
(Answer these questions to determine if you meet an exception to completing Section B. Note: Section B must always be completed for vehicles used by sole proprietors, partners, or other more than 5% owners or related persons.)

	Yes	No
34 Do you maintain a written policy statement that prohibits all personal use of vehicles, including commuting, by your employees?		
35 Do you maintain a written policy statement that prohibits personal use of vehicles, except commuting, by your employees? (See instructions for vehicles used by corporate officers, directors, or 1% or more owners.)		
36 Do you treat all use of vehicles by employees as personal use?		
37 Do you provide more than five vehicles to your employees and retain the information received from your employees concerning the use of the vehicles?		
38 Do you meet the requirements concerning qualified automobile demonstration use (see instructions)?		

Note: If your answer to 34, 35, 36, 37, or 38 is "Yes," you need not complete Section B for the covered vehicles.

Part VI Amortization

(a) Description of costs	(b) Date amortization begins	(c) Amortizable amount	(d) Code section	(e) Amortization period or percentage	(f) Amortization for this year
39 Amortization of costs that begins during your 1991 tax year:					

40 Amortization of costs that began before 1991	40	
41 Total. Enter here and on "Other Deductions" or "Other Expenses" line of your return.	41	

156

Form 4562 is the form most likely to send you running to an accountant. Depreciation rules are hard to understand. But if you only buy $10,000 or less of tangible property (such as computers and desks) a year for your business, you can usually deduct the expenses fully in Part I (Section 179 Expenses). This form also covers your automobile expenses.

---

home-based businesses don't take the deduction because they fear they'll be audited.

To qualify for the deduction, you must use an area or room of your home regularly and exclusively for business. "Regular use" is use on a continuing basis. Occasional or incidental use of your home office won't cut it, even if you don't use the space for anything else.

"Exclusive use" means just that. If you use the office for any personal activity, it doesn't qualify. Some "personal" furnishings, such as TVs and sofas, are off-limits for your home office—even though a regular business office may have these things.

The most accurate way to calculate the business portion of your home is to divide the square feet in the office by the total square feet of your home. If the rooms in your home are of roughly equal size, you also can divide one by the number of rooms in your home to arrive at the percentage.

Expenses you can deduct include the business percentage of:

- Rent
- Mortgage interest
- Utilities and services, such as electricity, heat, trash removal and cleaning services
- Depreciation of the value of your house
- Home security systems
- Repairs, maintenance and permanent improvement costs for your house

Keep in mind, if you itemize deductions on your tax return, you still can deduct the non-business portion of your mortgage interest on Schedule A as you deduct the business portion on Schedule C (which is for profit and loss from business). It's to your advantage to deduct some of your home-office costs on Schedule C, because that deduction reduces your self-employment tax as well as your income tax.

Remember, you can't use home-office expenses if they put you in the red. They can't be used to help create a tax loss.

Auto Expenses

If you work from your home, you can deduct mileage for any business purpose. This is true even if you don't qualify for the home-office deduction. If you work from an office outside the home, however, you can't deduct mileage for commuting to the office.

You can calculate auto expenses using the standard-mileage rate or the actual-cost method. Either way, you'll need to keep a mileage log. You'll also need to record your car's mileage at the beginning and end of the year.

You may not have a choice of methods in some circumstances. If you lease your car, or you use more than one vehicle in your business, you must use the actual-cost method. But if you use a second car only occasionally for business, you can still use the standard-mileage rate.

Otherwise, which method is better for you depends on several factors:

- The first year you buy a car is usually the optimal time to use the actual-cost method.
- If you plan to use the car less than 50 percent for business, that restricts how quickly you can write the car off. You're probably better off using the standard-mileage rate.
- The more expensive the car, the better using the actual-cost method is likely to be.
- Living in an area with high auto insurance rates or steep automobile taxes may tip the scales in favor of the actual-cost method.

To use the standard-mileage rate, merely multiply your annual mileage by the current year's mileage rate. It's the easiest method in terms of record keeping, but it may not yield the highest deduction.

As the name implies, the actual-cost method measures what it really costs you to operate your car, rather than using a rate that approximates the cost. For this method, you must keep receipts for all automobile expenses, including

gas, maintenance and repairs, insurance, taxes, loan interest and depreciation of the car's cost.

If you lease the car, deduct the lease payments instead of the depreciation and interest. How much you can deduct for a car lease may be limited for more expensive models. If you use the car for both business and personal reasons, calculate the percentage of business miles and deduct that percentage of your costs.

There are limits to how much of your car's value you may write off each year. For details of the exact amount you can depreciate, get a current copy of I.R.S. Publication 917.

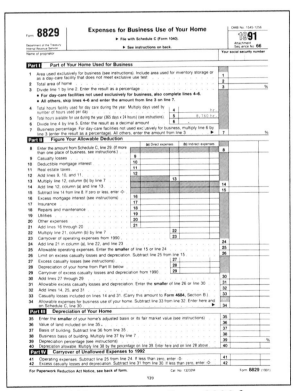

New on 1991 returns was Form 8829 for deducting home-office expenses. The form should help clear up any confusion for people who deduct some of their home's value, mortgage payments and taxes as business expenses and some as itemized deductions on Schedule A. One of the most complicated aspects of Form 8829 is subtracting the value of the land your home sits on from the basis you use for figuring depreciation. Checking with your county auditor or tax assessor's office could help here.

Self-Employment Tax

If your business is a sole proprietorship or a partnership, you must pay a self-employment tax for social security and Medicare in addition to ordinary income tax. The self-employment tax works out to nearly double what an employee pays for those taxes. That's because the employer picks up the other half. If your business is a corporation and you're technically an employee of the corporation, you pay the employee share and the corporation pays the employer share.

The self-employment tax can come as a big surprise to you in April if you didn't count on it from the beginning of the tax year. Taxes are easy to ignore your first year in business. The Internal Revenue Service expects you to pay estimated income taxes four times a year if you're self-employed. And if you owe more than $500 come April, you could be subject to a penalty.

To avoid the penalty and unpleasant surprises, it's best to put aside a third to a half of your net income from the business to cover federal, state and local taxes. The one-third should cover income taxed in the 15 percent federal income tax bracket (the other 18 percent is for self-employment and state and local taxes). You should withhold half of income that's likely to be taxed in the 28 percent bracket.

Contractors and Employees

When your work load gets so heavy that you need to hire help, which kind of help you hire has tax consequences. Hiring independent contractors rather than employees saves your paying the employer's share of social security and other payroll taxes and worker's compensation. Plus, it gives you more flexibility to deal with ups and downs in your business. How you handle the work arrangement, however, makes a difference in whether the Internal Revenue Service recognizes your relationship as that of a contractor or that of an employer.

Here are some key points to consider in deciding the difference:

■ Workers who come to your office and use your equipment are more likely to be considered employees. Those who work from their own offices with their own equipment are more

likely to be considered contractors.

■ Contractors generally set their own hours. Employees work on schedules determined by the employer.

■ Contractors generally submit bills or invoices for payment. Employees get paychecks.

Professional Help

Running a business of any size means filling out fairly complex tax forms. Smaller desktop design and publishing concerns can often get by without seeking professional help with their taxes. If you have employees or you're incorporated, you're more likely to need professional help. Some questions to ask yourself are:

■ How much would you have to pay someone else to do your taxes? If you devoted the time you're spending doing taxes to other areas of the business, would you make more than that?

■ How organized are your receipts, auto mileage log and other records? If they're a mess, you'll pay dearly for an accountant to straighten them out. If they're in good shape, it shouldn't take long to prepare your return.

If you decide on professional help, your options include independent tax preparers, tax preparation services, accountants and enrolled agents.

Certified Public Accountants are generally the most expensive option. But C.P.A.s have the advantage of being able to offer comprehensive business-planning services that the other options don't provide. Small- or medium-size firms are most likely to be familiar with issues that concern you as a small business. If you have a home office, find out how many of the C.P.A.'s clients also have home offices. C.P.A.s can help you with a broad range of issues besides taxes, including setting up a bookkeeping system and more complex areas of business and financial planning. For this reason, they may be your best all-around solution.

If you only want tax advice, enrolled agents may be your best option. They generally charge less than C.P.A.s. But they're required to pass a two-day exam given by the U.S. Treasury Department and then attend twenty-four to thirty hours a year of tax courses. In addition, many are former I.R.S. employees, so they know a lot about taxes and can provide year-round tax planning.

Franchise tax services and independent tax preparers are the cheapest option. But they may be less familiar with unusual tax situations than C.P.A.s or E.A.s. And they usually aren't around for year-round tax advice.

Using Your Computer to Manage Your Business

Besides earning money for you directly, your computer also can save you money by making your business more efficient. Handling records, invoices and other routine business matters on the computer is sensible for many desktop designer and publishers.

But it's important to keep in mind that the idea is to make keeping records as easy and as inexpensive as possible, not to get everything on the computer merely for the sake of looking modern. Surprisingly, some designers who use computers to serve clients still use paper to handle their own books. If you've always used a paper system and it works for you, there's not much point in changing. You don't have to constantly back up a paper bookkeeping system.

If you choose a compromise, you can still computerize some simple aspects of your business, such as creating model invoice and estimate templates on your word processing software. Then you can use a handy pocket calculator to do the rest.

Bookkeeping and Accounting Needs

If you want to use your computer for business management, the tasks you can automate include:

- Tracking billable hours by project and client
- Recording income and expenses
- Tax preparation
- Billing
- Estimating
- Tracking accounts receivable and payable
- Employee time records and payroll taxes
- Check-writing and bank account management

Checklist for Tax Planning

- □ Is your computer in a business office or qualified home office? If not, document percentage of business use.
- □ Can you deduct the entire cost of your computer or other equipment the first year?
- □ Do you have a home office or outside office?
- □ If a home office, does it qualify for deductions by being used regularly and exclusively for business?
- □ Should you deduct auto expenses using the standard-mileage rate or actual-cost method?
- □ Are you putting aside enough to cover what you'll owe in taxes? (To keep self-employment and other income taxes from coming as a surprise, put aside a third to a half of your net income.)

- Financial reporting, such as preparing balance sheets and cash flow projections
- Specialized reports, such as annual analysis of revenue and profitability broken down by client, type of work or employee

Various kinds of software handle one, several or all of these tasks. Generally, the more the software can do, the more complicated and expensive it will be. Your primary options include:

- *Spreadsheet programs, such as Excel, Quicken, Works and Lotus 1-2-3.* You can use them to handle many of the tasks, such as tracking billable hours, recording receipts and expenditures, and estimating. They don't have such bookkeeping functions built in, but you can customize them to fit your business. Even if you don't know how to customize the spreadsheet yourself, you may be able to buy or borrow templates that will do the job. One drawback is that spreadsheets don't provide invoicing or reporting, and it may be difficult to import the information to your word processor in a form that's easy to convert to an invoice.

■ *Checkbook programs, such as Quicken and Managing Your Money, which are basically computerized versions of your business checkbook.* The programs help you write and print checks and keep the account balance up-to-date. They also handle simple expense and income records, balance sheets, profit-and-loss statements, and accounts payable and receivable. Advantages are that they're cheap (around $50) and easy to use. Disadvantages are that they have trouble tracking cash transactions and don't help with tracking billable hours, preparing taxes or invoicing.

■ *Tax preparation software such as MacInTax, TaxCut and TurboTax, annual versions of which contain updated, step-by-step guidance in preparing business and personal taxes.* They're like having a tax preparation service in a box. A drawback is that there may not be a version for your state taxes.

■ *Timekeeping and billing programs.* Programs such as TimeSlips help you track what you've spent on each project for each client, then prepare the invoices. They do limited things, but they do them well. A more designer-specific version is DesignSoft, which costs around $200 and tracks billable hours and expenses, but doesn't do other accounting functions.

■ *General accounting software, which handles most accounting and business needs—from tracking billable hours to generating invoices and reports.* Costs range from less than $100 to several thousand dollars. Even low-end programs can be used to generate invoices, estimates and financial reports. But lower-cost programs don't track billable hours.

■ *Agency-specific software, such as Clients and Profits, Quintessentials and DesignSoft, which are designed specifically for ad agencies and design studios.* These programs have the most features and are the most closely tailored to your business needs. Clients and Profits and Quintessentials cost more than $2,000 and combine the ability to track billable hours with most other bookkeeping and accounting functions.

The choice that's best for you depends on several factors. For example, what do you really need? Is your goal to have the maximum amount of information at your fingertips or merely to increase the efficiency of your operation? If efficiency is your goal, does it make sense to spend days or weeks learning to use software to manage bookkeeping and accounting? How much time do you spend keeping records now? How much is your time worth? Will you really save money in the long run by automating everything instead of turning to an accountant?

Are you already familiar with checkbook, personal finance, spreadsheet or database programs that could be converted to handling aspects of your business? If so, that may be the fastest, and therefore cheapest, way to go.

Contracts: Protecting Yourself

Ideally, you would always have the protection of a written contract for every job you do. A contract dispels any confusion between you and a client, because both sides' expectations are right there in black and white. And the agreement gives you clearly documented rights if your client doesn't pay. But most jobs get done without a formal contract. And most times, that isn't a problem. A handshake is the only guarantee you usually need.

If you don't have a formal contract, at least have some documentation to show you've been hired for the job. That way, if the client has a change of heart after authorizing you to start work, you have something to prove you're owed money for the project. A letter or purchase order written by you or by the client will do.

Even if you have a contract, enforcing it in court can be a costly proposition. So every deal should also pass the smell test. If the job or the client seems fishy, back out diplomatically or make sure you get some kind of payment up front.

There's no law that says you must treat every prospective client the same. Some desktop designers and publishers have different payment policies for new and established customers. Established customers might get thirty days to pay their bills, new customers might get fifteen. Or new customers might automatically be required to sign a contract and provide a percentage of the estimated cost as a deposit. But such policies are often a luxury available only to businesses with an established clientele, since they can turn off too many new prospects.

In any case, it's a good idea to limit your exposure with a new client. And don't accept a second project until you get paid for the first one.

Protecting Your Rights

Getting bills paid is only part of the importance behind contractural relationships. The other part is establishing ownership of the work being done. Protect the copyright to the art you produce, if not for pride in your work, then merely for economic issues.

The key question you face is: Who owns the work, you or the client? The answer usually is you. Even though the client commissions you to create work, you own the copyright for it unless you surrender that right in a written contract. If there's no paper, you own the copyright, and all the client gets is permission to use the work once.

If you sign a contract, avoid yielding all rights. That way, you can stipulate an additional payment for future use of the artwork. If you sign away all rights in a work-for-hire arrangement, you also surrender your right to use the designs you create in your own promotional material. Even if you have no written contract, you may want to specify in your invoice that you retain the right to use the work for self-promotion and the right to payment for future uses of the work. If you confer rights in a contract, make sure you specify exactly which rights you confer. And make sure the contract addresses both mechanicals and disks when appropriate.

A corollary issue is whether the client has a right to alter the design without your consent. This is a money issue as well as an ego issue. You don't want someone else tampering with your product. And if the client decides to do some tweaking in the future, you want to be the one paid to tweak. This is an especially important issue for computer design, since it's much easier to alter work on disk than to redo mechanicals. This is one reason you may want to submit your work as mechanicals rather than on disk or by modem. That makes it much like-

Contract Checklist

It's relatively easy to develop a boilerplate contract to keep on your computer and customize as needed. You may want to consult a lawyer to help you prepare your standard contract, but it's not necessary. You may also want to consider investing $50 to $100 in one of the legal software packages on the market. In addition to a model client contract, such software may include other forms you can use, such as a license for intellectual property and work-for-hire agreements to use when you contract for work.

National organizations for artists and designers also offer members model contracts. Some are rather lengthy and may put off clients because they're written solely from the designer's standpoint. But they can at least be a start for you.

Basic things your contract should cover include:

- [ ] Description of the job
- [ ] When the work is due, allowing a grace period beyond which the contract becomes void
- [ ] Payment terms
- [ ] Interest or penalty to be paid on overdue bills
- [ ] Who owns the copyright to the work you produce
- [ ] Which rights are conferred to the client
- [ ] Whether the work can be altered without your consent
- [ ] An estimate of how much the job will cost and what happens if it goes over budget (such as a percentage above the budget you can go before needing additional authorization from the client)
- [ ] Provisions for extra charges, if any, for revisions
- [ ] Terms on how out-of-pocket expenses like printing or service bureau charges will be handled—i.e., as part of your bill and subject to a markup, or billed directly to the client

lier the client will come back to you for revisions. Remember, unless you've signed away your rights, you own the disk and the artwork.

Standing up for your rights could make your clients mad. How far you want to press the issue is a decision you can make based on the situation. But you should at least get to make the choice. And the only way to ensure that is not to sign away your rights.

Resources

Organizations

American Institute of Graphic Arts
1059 Third Avenue
New York, NY 10021
(212) 752-0813

Association of Desktop Publishers
P.O. Box 881667
San Diego, CA 92168-1667
(619) 279-2116

Boston Computer Exchange
P.O. Box 1177
Boston, MA 02103
(800) 262-6399
(GO BCE on CompuServe)

Graphic Artists Guild
11 West 20th Street
New York, NY 10011
(212) 463-7759

The International Design by Electronics
Association
(I.D.E.A.)
244 East 58th Street
New York, NY 10022

National Association of Desktop Publishers
Museum Wharf
300 Congress Street
Boston, MA 02210
(617) 426-2885

Publications

Advertising Age
740 Rush Street
Chicago, IL 60611
(312) 649-5200

Adweek
49 East 21st Street
New York, NY 10010
(212) 529-5500

Aldus Magazine
411 First Avenue South
Seattle, WA 98104
(Free to registered owners of FreeHand,
PageMaker and Persuasion)

Artist's Market
Writer's Digest Books
1507 Dana Avenue
Cincinnati, OH 45207
(513) 531-2222

Business Week
McGraw-Hill Publishing
1221 Avenue of the Americas
New York, NY 10020
(800) 635-1200

Cut & Paste
Data Search Publications
P.O. Box 363
Valley Cottage, NY 10989
(800) 745-4037

Desktop Communications
P.O. Box 941745
Atlanta, GA 30341

Encyclopedia of Associations
Gale Research Co.
Book Tower
Detroit, MI 48226
(313) 961-2242

Forbes
60 Fifth Avenue
New York, NY 10011

Fortune
1271 Avenue of the Americas
Rockefeller Center
New York, NY 10011
(800) 621-8000

Gale Directory of Publications
Gale Research Co.
Book Tower
Detroit, MI 48226
(313) 961-2242

Home Office Computing
P.O. Box 51344
Boulder, CO 80321-1344
(800) 288-7812

How: Ideas & Techniques in Graphic Design
1507 Dana Avenue
Cincinnati, OH 45207
(513) 531-2222

InfoWorld
P.O. Box 1172
Skokie, IL 60076
(708) 647-7925

MacUser
P.O. Box 56986
Boulder, CO 80321
(800) 622-8387

MacWeek
P.O. Box 1766
Riverton, NJ 08077-7366
(609) 461-2100
(Free to qualified subscribers)

Macworld
P.O. Box 54529
Boulder, CO 80323-4529

O'Dwyer's Directory of Public Relations Firms
J.R. O'Dwyer Co. Inc.
271 Madison Avenue
New York, NY 10016
(212) 679-2471

PC Publishing
P.O. Box 5050
Des Plaines, IL 60019-9162
(Free to qualified subscribers)

PC World
P.O. Box 55029
Boulder, CO 80322-5029
(800) 234-3498

Personal Publishing
P.O. Box 3019
Wheaton, IL 60189
(800) 727-6937

PRINT
104 Fifth Avenue
Ninth floor
New York, NY 10011-6998
(212) 463-0600

Publish
P.O. Box 55400
Boulder, CO 80322
(800) 274-5116

Standard Directory of Advertising Agencies
National Register Publishing Co.
3002 Glenview Road
Wilmette, IL 60091
(708) 256-6067

Standard Periodical Directory
Oxbridge Communications Inc.
150 Fifth Avenue
New York, NY 10011
(212) 741-0231

Suppliers (Fonts, Clip Art, Paper)

3G Graphics, Inc.
(Electronic clip art)
(800) 456-0234

Adobe Systems
(Fonts and electronic clip art)
(800) 833-6687

Artbeats
(Electronic clip art)
(714) 881-1200

Bitstream, Inc.
(Fonts)
(800) 237-3335

Casady & Greene
(Fonts and electronic clip art)
(800) 359-4920

ClickArt
T/MakerCompany
(Electronic clip art)
(415) 962-0195

Clip Art Books
North Light Books
(Printed clip art)
(800) 289-0963

Cliptures
Dream Maker Software
(Electronic clip art)
(818) 353-2297

Comstock Desktop Photography
Comstock, Inc.
(Electronic stock photo library)
(212) 353-8686

Darkroom CD-ROM
Image Club Graphics
(Electronic stock photo library)
(800) 661-9410

Dover Pictorial Archive Books
Dover Publications
(Printed clip art)
(516) 294-7000

Dynamic Graphics
(309) 688-8800
(800) 255-8800 (orders only)

Emigre Fonts
(Fonts)
(800) 944-9021

The Font Company
(Fonts)
(602) 998-7964

Font Factory Fonts (for Laserjet)
The Font Factory
(214) 239-6085

FontHaus, Inc.
(Discount fonts)
(800) 942-9110

Fontek
Letraset
(Fonts)
(800) 343-8973

Fontographer
Altsys Corporation
(Font manipulation and design program)
(214) 680-2060

Hewlett-Packard Soft Fonts (for LaserJet)
Hewlett-Packard Company
(800) 538-8787

Image Club
(Fonts and electronic clip art)
(800) 661-9410

Linotype Library
(Fonts)
(800) 842-8721

Font/DA Juggler
Alsoft Corporation
(Font management utility)
(713) 353-1510

Monotype fonts
Monotype Typography
(Fonts)
(800) 666-6897

Norton Tools
Symantec
(Disk optimization and disk/file repair utility
for Mac and PC)
(800) 441-7234

Norton Utilities
Symantec
(Disk and file management utility for Mac
and PC)
(800) 441-7234

Ornate Typefaces
Ingrimayne Software
(219) 866-6241

Pantone Color Match Systems
Pantone, Inc.
(201) 935-5500

Paper Direct
(Offers free paper kit with hundreds of paper
and envelope samples with first $30 purchase
from catalog)
(800) 272-7377

Photo Gallery
NEC Technologies, Inc.
(Electronic stock photo library)
(508) 264-8000

PhotoFiles
GoldMind Publishing
(Electronic stock photo library)
(714) 687-3815

PostScript Type Sampler
Publishing Solutions
(Fonts)
(301) 424-3942

Precision Type
(Free type catalog)
(516) 864-1024

Professional Photography Collection
disc*Imagery*
(Electronic stock photo library)
(212) 675-8500

Publisher's Prism
InSight Systems
(Color separation program)
(800) 688-0250

Queblo
(Sample paper kit with free paper selection
guide, "The Wheel"; call for price)
(800) 253-9080

QuicKeys
CE Software
(Macro making utility)
(515) 224-1995

Suitcase II
Fifth Generation Systems
(Font management utility)
(504) 291-7221

Treacyfaces, Inc.
(Fonts)
(215) 896-0860

Trumatch Color Finder
(Digital four-color matching system)
Trumatch, Inc.
(212) 517-2237

Type Align
Emerald City Software
(Font manipulation and design program)
(415) 324-8080

TypeStyler
Broderbund Software
(Font manipulation and design program)
(800) 521-6263

Typographic Ornaments
The Underground Grammarian
(Fonts)
(609) 589-6477

Varityper Type Library
Tegra/Varityper
(Fonts)
(201) 887-8000

Ventura Color Extensions
Venture Software, Inc.
(Color publishing utilities for use with Ventura
Publisher)
(800) 822-8221

National Mail Order Houses

It would be impossible to list all the companies who sell this way. This is a sample to give you an idea of what is available; a listing here is *not* an endorsement of the company's products or services.

The Computer Buyer's Club (PC)
(800) 732-3396

The Computermill (PC)
(800) 800-5592

MacConnection
(800) 800-3333

MacDepot
(800) 222-2808

MacLand
(800) 888-8779

Mac's Place
(800) 367-4222

MacWarehouse
(800) 255-6227

PC Connection
(800) 243-8088

PC Zone
(800) 252-0286

Software Vendors (Draw, Paint, Layout and Image Editing Programs)

If no type of computer is specified for a particular software package, it is available for both Mac and PC systems. Not all programs for the PC may be available for both Windows and DOS, so you should check on availability and the correct current version of what you need.

Aldus PrePrint
Aldus Corporation
(206) 622-5500

Arts & Letters (PC)
Computer Support Corporation
(214) 661-8960

Canvas (Mac)
Deneba Software
(800) 622-6827

Color Studio (Mac)
Fractal Design
(408) 688-8800

CorelDRAW! (PC)
Corel
(800) 836-3729

Deluxe Paint (PC)
Electronic Arts
(800) 245-4525

Digital Darkroom (Mac)
Silicon Beach Software/Aldus Corporation
(619) 695-6956

Fractal Design Painter
Fractal Design Corporation
(408) 688-8800

FreeHand
Aldus Corporation
(206) 622-5500

Illustrator
Adobe Systems
(800) 833-6687

Lumena (PC)
Time Arts, Inc.
(415) 576-7722

MacDraw (Mac)
Claris Corporation
(800) 544-8554

MacPaint (Mac)
Claris Corporation
(800) 544-8554

Micrografx Designer (PC)
Micrografx, Inc.
(214) 234-1769

Micrografx Draw (PC)
Micrografx Windows Draw (PC)
Micrografx, Inc.
(214) 234-1769

Micrografx Picture Publisher (PC)
Micrografx, Inc.
(214) 234-1769

PageMaker
Aldus Corporation
(206) 622-5500

PC Paintbrush (PC)
Z-Soft
(800) 444-4780

Photoshop
Adobe Systems
(800) 833-6687

PhotoStyler
Aldus Corporation
(206) 622-5500

Picture Publisher (PC)
Micrografx, Inc.
(214) 234-1769

PixelPaint Professional
SuperMac Technology
(408) 245-2202

Professional Draw (PC)
Gold Disk, Inc.
(800) 465-3375

Publisher's Paintbrush (PC)
ZSoft
(800) 444-4780

QuarkXPress (Mac)
Quark, Inc.
(800) 356-9363
(A PC version is in development)

Ready,Set,Go! (Mac)
Manhattan Graphics
(800) 572-6533

Studio/8 (Mac)
Electronic Arts
(800) 245-4525

Studio/32 (Mac)
Electronic Arts
(800) 245-4525

SuperPaint (Mac)
Aldus Corporation
(206) 622-5500

Targa TIPS (PC)
Truevision
(317) 841-0332

UltraPaint (Mac)
Deneba Software
(800) 622-6827

Ventura Publisher (PC)
Ventura Software, Inc.
(800) 822-8221

Software Vendors (Business Applications)

Clients and Profits
Working Computer
P.O. Box 87
San Luis Rey, CA 92068
(619) 945-4334

DesignSoft
Highgate Cross & Cathey
124B South County Farm Road
Wheaton, IL 60187
(708) 653-2700

Managing Your Money
Meca Ventures
55 Walls Drive
Fairfield, CT 06430
(203) 256-5000

MYOB
22 Hill Road
Parsippany, NJ 07054
(201) 334-1154

Quicken
Intuit
P.O. Box 3014
Menlo Park, CA 94206
(800) 624-8742

Quintessentials
The Five A's
1 East 28th Street
New York, NY 10016
(212) 779-0713

Government Agencies

I.R.S. Tax Information and pamphlets
(800) 424-1040

Service Corps of Retired Executives
National Headquarters
409 3rd Street NW
Washington, D.C. 20416
(202) 653-6279

U.S. Small Business Administration
(800) 368-5855

Index

Improve your skills, learn a
new technique, with these additional
books from North Light